DECONSTRUCTED

An Insider's View of Illegal Immigration and the Building Trades

by Loren C. Steffy with Stan Marek

STONEY CREEK PUBLISHING
www.stoneycreekpublishing.com

Other Books by Loren C. Steffy

George P. Mitchell: Fracking, Sustainability,
and an Unorthodox Quest to Save the Planet

The Man Who Thought Like a Ship

Drowning in Oil: BP and Reckless Pursuit of Profit

With Chrysta Castañeda:
The Last Trial of T. Boone Pickens

Published by Stoney Creek Publishing
stoneycreekpublishing.com
in association with 30 Point Press
30point.com

Copyright © 2020 Loren C. Steffy

ISBN: 978-1-7340822-2-7
ISBN (ebook): 978-1-7340822-3-4
Library of Congress: 2020910835

Cover & interior design by Anton Ioukhnovets for 30 Point Press
Cover image: Getty Images
Printed in the United States

Contents

Notes on terminology

Throughout this book, we refer to those who enter the United States illegally as either "illegal immigrants" or "undocumented." We have avoided the more derogatory term "illegal alien," as well as using "illegal" as a noun. While people may have come to the country illegally, that alone is not what defines them. Many people have broken laws—by speeding or drinking under age, for instance—but they are not defined as "illegals." The same holds true for immigrants. In America, a person is not illegal, even if his or her actions or immigration status are.

– – – –

Stan Marek is referred to as "Stan" and his company as "Marek" or "Marek Brothers" to prevent confusion between the man and his business.

Foreword

By Stan Marek

When Loren and I first discussed writing a book about immigration and the construction industry, I thought hard about the risk and the reward. Taking an unpopular stance is not easy and exposing one's company to the threat of audits, blackballing by potential clients, or dozens of unknown consequences certainly concerned me.

But every time I visited a job site or had a company meeting with our field employees, I realized I would be letting them down if I did not make a stand for what is right for our company and our industry. We at Marek have spent decades building a trained, quality, hourly workforce. And sitting idly by while more and more fellow contractors adopt practices that move them further and further from a mutually beneficial employer/employee business model is not the answer. We know we have a broken system when the workers our industry needs are undocumented, and companies find ways to keep them "off the books." It's not fair to companies that play by the rules, and it's certainly detrimental to the legal workers who have seen their own wages and opportunities diminished.

Before I began my own career in construction, I watched scores of men enjoy a successful middle-class occupation in the company my dad and his brothers founded. Construction was an honorable career. The skill levels were high and the rewards for them were plentiful. To see this ethic being squandered is incredibly distasteful.

I don't blame contractors for moving away from employees who get hourly pay, benefits, training, and worker protection—although I wish they wouldn't. Ultimately, they are reacting to the realities of the marketplace, as all businesses do. I blame the federal government and, in particular, our elected officials who have refused to address this situation for more than three decades.

Most people believe our country's immigration system is broken. Their differences lie in how to fix it. While our politicians line up along party lines, America and Americans suffer. To me, the path to a solution is simple: Let's do what's best for America and our economy. If we approached the immigration mess in this way, we would find agreement somewhere in the middle. But that is somewhere our elected officials haven't been willing to go, opting rather to hide behind party loyalties on the far right and left.

As factions dig in, industries like construction scramble to find enough workers. We have tried, and tried hard, yet our American-born workers have been opting for other careers, leaving immigrants to fill the void. Many of them are not here legally because the demand for labor far exceeds the legal limitations of our immigration laws.

Those who seek a positive solution to our industry's shortage of skilled labor might find it in our high schools. Until the late 1960s, considering young graduates for trades jobs was a natural process. Only a handful of them headed to college. The rest went directly into a career, many of them choosing construction. When high schools eliminated craft training years ago, the natural pipeline dried up. Instead, the curriculum focused on preparation for college. Unfortunately, during this time, the dropout rate was hitting an all-time high in many schools.

Several contractors in Texas have taken the lead in establishing a vocational pipeline. They are working with school districts and community college systems to recruit juniors and seniors and offer them internships to learn a trade that will lead to a career in construction. Initial results have been positive, and it's a win for the kids as well as the schools and the industry. But for programs like this to work, we must fix our broken immigration system. The large number of undocumented people in our workforce depresses wages and opportunities. I propose a simple solution that I call "ID and Tax." This approach is basically an adult form of the Deferred Action for Childhood Arrivals (DACA) program and would give the undocumented legal status to participate as valued, tax-paying members of our construction community.

These issues are terribly important to me, as well as to our team at Marek. After eighty-plus years of providing a livelihood for thousands of workers and their families, we owe it to the next generation to give them the opportunity to preserve and pass down the same values and culture that built this company.

I am grateful to my wife, Reinnette, and our three children, Mike, Ben, and Elisabeth, for their patience and support as I've fought for sensible immigration reform and improved living and working conditions for immigrants. I have been blessed with wonderful role models: strong men and women with strong convictions—none stronger than my Dad, Ralph. He taught us all that business is about people and companies are strengthened by good people given the chance to do the right things. God bless us all and may we find a timely and sensible solution to our long-standing immigration impasse.

Preface

By Loren C. Steffy

Cars and trucks—mostly pickups—flow into the field behind the Knights of Columbus Hall in north Houston. The hall is old, but the event is older. For more than eighty years, the Marek Family of Companies—which started business in 1938 as Marek Brothers Sheetrock—has hosted a Christmas party for employees. Started by the grandsons of Czech immigrants, the company today is the largest specialty drywall and interiors installer in the southwestern U.S. In the final weeks of 2019, more than a thousand current and former employees lined up for a barbecue lunch followed by an awards ceremony that recognized long-time workers. More than three hundred of them have worked there for at least twenty years, and some for more than fifty.

As we walk across the field toward the hall, Stan Marek, the company's chief executive and the son of one of its founders, sweeps his hand across the sea of vehicles. "Look at how many of these trucks are new," he says. "This is what happens when you have real employees. They can afford to buy things like trucks and houses."

By "real" employees he means full-time hires on his payroll, not workers who are mischaracterized as independent contractors and doing piecework for anyone who needs them that day. The distinction is significant in the construction business. In the past twenty years, the industry has emerged as a flashpoint in the debate over immigration. These misclassified workers and the companies that hire them have upended decades of economic convention. Unlike Marek, many employers rely on undocumented immigrants because they are so easy to misclassify—and thus to marginalize. Their bosses see them as largely disposable, or at least interchangeable, paying them in cash, and providing no safety training, health benefits, or additional money for overtime. This keeps costs down but does little to build a skilled and reliable workforce, encourage loyalty, or provide financial security for the workers—or the companies themselves.

Stan has long believed construction companies' reliance on this system hurts workers and the industry. He suggested that I write this book to show how the impact of illegal immigration has eroded wages and degraded working conditions and quality in the industry. He also wanted a platform to illustrate his proposed "ID and Tax" solution. But it's outside the Knights of Columbus hall on an overcast December day that the point of everything Stan has worked tirelessly for hits home in the most basic way.

Employees who get a regular paycheck can verify their employment to a bank. That means they can apply for financing to buy a new truck. "Off-the-books" contractors working for cash must settle for whatever vehicle they can afford for the money they have in their pocket. Unknowingly, they underpin and perpetuate a shadow economy from which they have little chance to escape.

Stan talks a lot about the need for workers to be brought out of the shadows. The effort would require that they pay taxes on their income and, in turn, that their employers fund payroll taxes and workers' compensation insurance, as Marek does. The money that Stan pays employees begins a ripple that fans out across the economy. His workers have a verifiable source of regular income. This lets them finance a truck, sign a satellite TV contract, buy a house, or put in a pool. In other words, they participate fully in the economy.

In contrast, the estimated eleven million illegal immigrants who live in the United States work for cash in the shadow economy. They may buy groceries and electronics. Some may even manage to purchase homes. But their participation in mainstream economic activities is limited. They don't get the rewards of a steady paycheck or a retirement plan. At the same time, they extract a higher price on society in unanticipated ways. Rather than scheduling regular doctor visits, they may choose the emergency room for routine ailments—the most expensive form of medical care. Ultimately, local taxpayers foot the bill. In this case and in myriad other instances, the economy—and thus the country—doesn't receive the full benefit that it does from employees who work on the books, pay taxes, and contribute to the funding of their medical and other expenses. In Texas, about 24 percent of all construction workers are undocumented, the result of decades of immigration laws out of step with economic reality.

Illegal immigration stems from complex economic, legal, and political factors that many Americans don't understand. They've had little reason to delve into the intricacies or the origins. Most native-born citizens know only the romantic tales of ancestors, fighting in the Revolution or coming through Ellis Island, searching for a better life, and enduring perilous journeys and hard work before achieving financial stability and the American Dream.

Immigrants have long been the source of America's economic strength. Yet our immigration laws have always been ill-defined and arbitrary, based largely on the fears of the moment and aimed at limiting particular groups of people. These fears—and the sources of them—have ebbed and flowed over the decades. Today anxiety over immigration is omnipresent and it means that the United States has evolved from a country open to almost anyone to a country that few can come to legally. In fact, our borders can be closed to new arrivals with the stroke of a president's pen. As the coronavirus pandemic of 2020 engulfed the nation, President Donald Trump reacted by suspending almost all legal immigration to the United States, at least temporarily. What struck me, the more I talked to Stan over the course of writing this book, is that he is trying to bring a rational approach to a debate that has consistently shown little appetite for rationality.

The federal government has contributed to the confusion surrounding illegal immigration. Officials have enforced existing immigration laws poorly and inconsistently. This is partly because the government doesn't have the money or the resources to deport all eleven million illegal immigrants, as President George W. Bush noted in 2007. Even with more recent attempts to step up deportations—and with the feds' growing reliance on local law enforcement to assist and help pay for the initial arrests and detentions of undocumented immigrants—the government is doing little to reduce the number of undocumented people already in the country.

Some immigration foes argue that the cost and feasibility of mass deportations don't matter. They say that "illegal is illegal," and every undocumented immigrant should be rounded up and sent back to his or her country of origin. They seem to think their ancestors arrived "the right way," and today's undocumented immigrants are coming "the wrong way." In fact, immigrants at Ellis Island shared more in common with the Latinos showing up at the southern border than they do with those who receive visas. No one came to Ellis Island with permission. What changed was not the attraction of America for immigrants or the circumstances of their arrival, but the policies enacted by those who were already here.

Calls for mass deportations of illegal immigrants ignore economic reality. Beyond the prohibitive costs of processing so many people, removing millions of workers from the economy could stifle productivity and trigger a recession.

In the wake of the COVID-19 pandemic, when much of the U.S. economy was shuttered, the government designated workers in agriculture, food processing, and construction as "essential," regardless of their immigration status. Others lost their jobs and were left to fend for themselves without the social or economic safety nets provided for legal residents. Yet as the economy recovers, it may once again turn to immigrants—both legal and illegal—for some of the most vital services, just as the country has in the recovery from other disasters.

A rational approach to mending our inconsistent policies requires an economic solution to illegal immigration. Such a change would consider not just the costs of enforcement but also weigh the potential benefits of reform against the price of perpetuating a failing system and a shadow economy.

Focusing on the economics of illegal immigration makes sense because most immigrants who arrive illegally come in pursuit of an economic benefit: a job. Yet our immigration laws have never been based on economics. Nowhere is this more evident than in the Texas construction industry: Here a shortage of labor—legal or undocumented—has left the industry struggling to meet demand. Native-born applicants are not flooding job sites looking for construction work. Since the late 1990s, Stan and his company have actively recruited from high schools, community colleges, and even prisons, yet their efforts haven't attracted enough workers. Even today, despite Stan's efforts, most young Americans prefer jobs less strenuous than construction.

The construction industry in America stands out for its inextricable link to the immigration story. Many companies like Marek were founded by the descendants of immigrants and, from their earliest days, provided jobs for other immigrants. The work was hard, but the pay was good enough for those workers to earn a middle-class living and carve out their piece of the American Dream.

This book traces America's about-face from the welcoming arms of Ellis Island to the bitter rebuke of wall-building. It attempts to address many of the myths that immigration has spawned, and to put the current crisis of millions of undocumented immigrants living in a shadow economy ignored by lawmakers in the context of history. The story of the Marek family parallels this trajectory.

Stan Marek is not well known outside of Houston, but few individuals have worked harder to reform immigration policy. This book grows in part from his frustration that he hasn't been able to do more.

I first met Stan when I was writing a business column for the Houston Chronicle. He became a frequent source and a friend, and when we talked about doing a book together, I jumped at the chance. He has proven to be a wonderful writing partner because he gave me the freedom to shape the manuscript, offering only minor suggestions along the way.

The result is a book that explores the economic issues surrounding immigration as interpreted through the eyes and world view of a man who has witnessed the changes to his workforce—and his industry—firsthand. Stan is not a cold, calculating businessman, interested only in finding the cheapest labor. He wants his company to succeed, and he's proud of its accomplishments. But he also is a humanitarian who cares about the people who work for him— many of whom, like construction workers for generations, are immigrants. I've gotten to know a lot of these people. The respect they have for Stan and his cousins, Bruce and Paul, reflects their gratitude for being treated as valued members of the Marek team. The company's ideals are important to Stan. He emphasizes that throughout its history, Marek has operated on the belief that taking care of employees ensures the success of the business.

Stan wants to build a system that treats everyone fairly and provides opportunity and dignity for all who lift a hammer for a living. He'd hoped for comprehensive reform in which undocumented workers already in the country could find a pathway to citizenship and new arrivals could be welcomed and allowed to work to keep our economy functioning efficiently. However, as the immigration debate has ground on, Stan has lowered his expectations. Now, he would settle for a system that identifies undocumented workers, takes them out of the shadows, and allows them to participate fully in the economy without fear of arrest or deportation. He calls the system "ID and Tax." It would create a level playing field among construction companies by bringing immigrant workers onto payrolls and establishing more stable employment for the workers. It would improve security by identifying who's in the country and ensure that they and their employers pay all appropriate taxes.

As Stan's workers ate barbecue at the Christmas lunch, he outlined his latest efforts in fighting for rational immigration reform. Most of those in the hall already knew that Stan met regularly with U.S. congressmen and state lawmakers, that he had funded organizations to change immigration policy, and that he frequently wrote guest newspaper columns advocating reform. He told them about this book and a companion video series, "The Rational Middle of Immigration." He and other local business leaders are supporting the initiative to broaden public understanding of immigration. He said he hopes new knowledge will usher in political and social change.

After the lunch, a longtime Latino employee approached Stan. "Thank you," he said, "for all you're doing for us." I didn't know if he meant immigrants, Latinos, construction workers, or Marek employees. He could have meant all four.

Section I

From Ellis Island to Illegality

1

Firings and ICE

On a Monday morning in 2009, the phone chirped on Stan Marek's desk, and he snapped up the receiver. It was still early, and he wasn't expecting any calls, let alone visitors. On the other end, the front-desk receptionist sounded nervous. Half a dozen men in dark windbreakers had filed into the lobby moments earlier and demanded to see the owner of the company. They looked like FBI agents, she said. The company Stan runs with his two cousins was founded by their fathers, and this family business has prided itself on following the rules for more than eighty years. He knew the men in the lobby weren't from the FBI, but he also knew they were from the federal government, and he wouldn't like what they were going to say.

Stan told the receptionist he would be right there. He sighed as he set the receiver down and glanced out the plate-glass window behind his desk. He had a corner office, but it didn't offer much to look at. Other CEOs in Houston stared down from lofty skyscrapers, but his view was only one story off the ground and overlooked an area where his employees were loading drywall onto trucks to be sent to job sites. Beyond that were train tracks, then the Interstate 610 loop that encircles downtown Houston. The Marek offices were on land that his father and uncles bought in 1960. Stan oversaw a construction enterprise, known simply by his family name, Marek, that stretched across the Southwest and employed more than two thousand people. He was proud of the family company, which he and his cousins continued to build. He wondered if the men in the windbreakers waiting in his lobby could appreciate the sacrifices three generations of Mareks had made to get to this point.

Stan walked down the chrome-railed staircase, across the breeze-way his construction crews used as a loading dock in the mornings when they arrived for their shifts and badged himself into the main building. He was five feet, eight inches tall, and although he was in his late sixties, he didn't look like it. His hair was graying, but he walked quickly, like someone who still had a lot to get done. Across the expansive, two-story lobby, he could see the agents. On the back of their jackets, in big yellow letters, was one word: ICE— the acronym for Immigration and Customs Enforcement. As Stan approached the agents, he knew this was the moment he and a great many other employers in Houston had been dreading.

ICE was formed as a division of the Department of Homeland Security in the wake of the September 11, 2001, terrorist attacks. The assaults on U.S. soil reshaped a host of government programs and created several new federal agencies. ICE combined the old U.S. Customs Service and the U.S. Immigration and Naturalization Service; Congress infused it with a unique combination of civil and criminal authority.

As Stan walked toward them, the ICE agents turned to face him. The administration of President Barack Obama, who took office in 2009, had promised a new "get tough" policy on illegal immigration. It focused less on rounding up undocumented workers and instead directed government enforcement efforts at the companies that employed them. Except for agriculture, no industry in Texas employed more undocumented workers than the construction business, and Marek was one of the biggest specialty subcontractors in town. It got its start hanging drywall and later expanded into carpentry, flooring and painting—basically any interior construction work that a developer required. Marek's size may have put it on ICE's radar for one of the agency's first workplace audits in Houston, or it may have been Stan's frequent calls to senators, representatives, and Obama administration officials stressing the need for immigration reform. "Everybody told me I was too big of a target," Stan recalled. Other employers who publicly called for immigration reform felt that ICE targeted them unfairly for audits, too, said Jacob Monty, a lawyer in Houston who works with companies on immigration issues. "Employers that speak out, they sometimes get retaliated against by ICE," Monty said. "And the public often misunderstands and thinks 'Oh, they just want cheap labor.' I know Stan, and that's not what he wants."

Nevertheless, Stan, a lifelong Republican, now found himself targeted by a Democratic administration, and he couldn't help but wonder as he approached the agents in his lobby if his vocal support for immigration reform was to blame for what he knew was about to happen. As he shook the lead agent's hand, the man said: "Mr. Marek, we're going to do an I-9 audit." I-9s are officially known as Employment Eligibility Verification forms. Employers are supposed to complete one for each worker, verifying the person's identity and eligibility to work in the United States. ICE wanted to audit Marek's records to see if the company had any employees who were in the country illegally.

Stan felt a lump rise in his throat. Marek tried to confirm the citizenship of workers, but it wasn't as easy as it sounded. By law, employees could provide as many as thirty-two different kinds of identification, and it was difficult to assess the accuracy of each. Besides, the most common form of ID, the Social Security card, is among the easiest to forge.

"How long do we have to get the information?" Stan asked.

"Seventy-two hours," the agent replied.

"Well, do you mind if I get with my attorney?"

"Sure, but you've got seventy-two hours and then we want to see your I-9s," the agent said.

"Well," Stan stammered as the magnitude of the task sank in, "we've got a lot of people."

"Well, you've got seventy-two hours," the agent said again. He turned and headed for the door, and the other agents followed.

Stan returned to his office and called his attorney, Charles Foster. Foster had been practicing immigration law in Houston for some forty years. He grew up in McAllen, Texas, on the Mexican border, working side by side with immigrants, both legal and illegal. As a lawyer, he'd served as an adviser on immigration to presidents Obama and George W. Bush, as well as aiding Republican and Democratic candidates including Mitt Romney, Jeb Bush, and Hillary Clinton.[1] His firm, Foster LLP, is one of the largest immigration law firms in the country.

Foster convinced ICE to extend Marek's deadline by a couple of weeks and the company complied. It was a big task: The agency wanted I-9s going back three years, which meant producing some three thousand documents. The agents also wanted to see the IDs each worker had presented at the time they were hired. The Social Security card or other identification had to appear authentic— Marek couldn't be expected to detect a good forgery, but the card had to have the correct numbers in the proper configurations, and it had to *look* like a real Social Security card. If Marek had accepted any obvious forgeries, company executives could face fines or even jail time. Marek used an electronic government system known as E-Verify to confirm its employees' immigration status. E-Verify, though, wasn't fool-proof. If workers had what appeared to be a valid ID, it would pass the E-Verify check. Employers like Marek could follow all the rules and still wind up hiring undocumented workers.

The ICE agents returned with the results of their audit a few months later. All of the I-9s had been filled out correctly, which meant Marek wouldn't face penalties. But ICE had found that about two hundred workers had improper documentation. Their identification didn't match Social Security Administration records. The agency gave the employees ninety days clear up the discrepancies. If they didn't, the agents told Stan, he would have to fire them.

Marek is a privately held company—the only shareholders are Stan and his cousins, Bruce and Paul Marek—and it's the sort of business that values employee longevity. It routinely holds company rallies in the two-story lobby where it honors long-time employees for their service: Tenures of thirty to forty years are common. Stan knew each of the two hundred workers, and he met with them individually to tell them about the ICE audit. Some had been with him for decades. They owned homes and had raised families in Houston. Marek provided them with health benefits and 401(k) retirement plans, and it paid their payroll taxes. But most of the two hundred, it turned out, were in the U.S. illegally. Some simply admitted their immigration status when Stan confronted them, others made up reasons why they couldn't go to the Social Security office. Still others said they would but didn't. Ultimately, Stan had to let most of the two hundred go.

Stan Marek sees himself as a champion of the working man. In an era in which more and more Americans earn a living by sitting in front of a computer screen, he still believes that people who work with their hands and use tools to make things should be able to earn a middle-class income. He isn't oblivious to the changing workplace, and he recognizes that the demographics of his industry have shifted—in fact, he watched it happen. He knows that progress means businesses and industries must change. Marek, in fact, prides itself on embracing cutting edge technology— it's testing virtual reality googles on the job site and has its own drone. The company seeks to cultivate a dedicated and diverse workforce. From the time of its founding, Marek has relied on first- and second-generation immigrants from a wide range of countries.

But in some ways, Stan's views on the workplace remain decidedly old-fashioned. He believes a good employer takes care of his employees, and the employees, in turn, take care of the company by doing good work. Stan's father taught him that lesson when he handed Stan the reins of the business in the early 1980s. Back then, the traditional employment model in construction started with the general contractor, who would oversee a building project. The general contractor hired subcontractors, like Marek, who had a workforce of employees who received hourly pay, overtime, benefits, workers' compensation insurance, and job training. The subcontractor paid payroll taxes and provided I-9s on all its workers.

In the past three decades, however, the model has changed. Fewer subcontractors have their own workers. Instead, they hire laborers they treat as independent contractors and pay them for piecework. In the drywall business, for example, these independent workers are paid by foot of wallboard hung, not by the hour. They receive no overtime, benefits, workers' compensation insurance, or employer-funded training. That leaves many workers earning poverty-level wages and no overtime pay for longer hours. The workers pay no taxes, have no insurance if they're injured on the job, and essentially have no career path. They will never be promoted to a supervisor position because those jobs are held by the subcontractor who hired them. For many illegal immigrant workers, this is the only employment option. The arrangement has created a system that hurts the workers, leads to more accidents, mistakes and shoddy workmanship, and ultimately under-mines the industry's future.

Stan has seen more of Marek's competitors choose this path. Many subcontractors' offices are staffed by a few white-collar employees who manage a virtual workforce of low-paid, often un-skilled and ever-shifting laborers. Many of these workers are in the country illegally.

Stan thought about the irony of the situation. Marek believed in paying its employees well, providing workers' compensation insurance in case they were injured, and offering the training they needed to do a quality job while making their job sites safer. Marek's workers all had income taxes withheld from their checks, and they all paid into Social Security. Even if they had stayed on his payroll, the two hundred workers he had to let go would never receive the benefits of their Social Security contribution because the Social Security numbers they submitted to Marek were inval-id. In a strange way, they were actually strengthening the perpet-ually under-funded Social Security entitlement program for mil-lions of other retirees by paying in but not taking out.

Stan felt badly for the workers he dismissed. What would happen to them? Would they be deported, forced to return to a coun-try many of them hadn't seen in decades? How would they pro-vide for their families? After all, some had children who were U.S. citizens. By firing them, had he set in motion events that would tear families apart?

Even though Stan had to let them go, many of the workers re-mained loyal to him and stayed in touch. None of them was deport-ed. Instead, over the next few weeks, or in some cases, the next few days, they found other jobs. After all, these were skilled laborers who had been trained by Marek, which had a reputation for quality. They knew how to do the job right. The companies that hired them, though, did things differently. In most cases, the new employers paid five dollars an hour less than Marek paid. Their workers received no health or retirement benefits. No taxes were drawn from their paychecks because in most cases the workers were paid in cash or as independents who were responsible for their own taxes—they received a 1099 Form from the Internal Revenue Service for their wages, rather than a W-2, if there were any record of their pay at all.[2] There was no accident insurance or paid overtime, and the local emergency room was their health care provider.

The turn of events enraged Stan. On a purely business level, the employees he'd nurtured and trained were now competing against him at a lower cost. At the same time, these workers were more likely to become a greater burden on society than when they had worked for him. And the companies who hired them were rewarded for perpetuating a shadow economy created by decades of misguided immigration policy. Stan had witnessed the slow erosion of his part of the construction industry from one that offered careers to one that offered essentially day labor. He knew the industry couldn't continue on this path without paying a price in lost quality and compromised safety. He wanted something better for workers and for his industry, and he was determined to change immigration policy.

– – – –

Stan's father, Ralph Marek, founded the family business with his siblings, John and Bill, in 1938. The three brothers had grown up in Texas, the grandsons of Czech immigrants who entered the U.S. in the late 1800s through Galveston, a coastal city that served as the Texas version of Ellis Island. Thousands of Europeans followed a similar path to Texas in the years after the Civil War, chasing their dreams of a better life. Back then, the construction industry was full of nearly identical stories. Some of the biggest companies in the business were founded by immigrants just a few generations removed from the present. "So many of these big companies around the United States have very American-sounding names, but in so many cases they were founded by Irish immigrant families or Norwegian immigrant families," said Pat Kiley, a Houston management consultant who has spent decades working with construction firms.

In the three generations since Stan's ancestors arrived, however, America's views of immigration—and the immigration policy that reflected those views—had changed dramatically. Stan had seen those changes himself. In Texas, the 1980s began with an oil boom that fueled a building surge. A devastating collapse of oil prices followed, taking real estate with it. Hundreds of banks and savings and loans across the state failed, decimating lending for new projects. People were desperate for secure jobs, and young men who had made a living in construction turned to other professions. By the time the economy rebounded in the 1990s, the ranks of builders increasingly were filled with Latino workers, many of whom, no doubt, had come to the country illegally. Just like Stan's ancestors, they embraced the hard work of construction as a means of building a life in America.

Since then, wave after wave of illegal immigrants has upset the economics of the construction business. The 2008 recession, stricter immigration policies, sluggish economic growth, and a profound labor shortage put Stan and his company at a disadvantage. Many of his competitors no longer bothered to hire full-time workers. Instead, they used labor brokers—who delivered legions of "independent contractors" to complete work on a job-by-job basis. Neither the brokers nor the workers they hired were employees, so construction companies weren't required to ask key questions: Were the workers citizens? Were taxes withheld from their paychecks? Were they paid overtime? Were they covered by workers' compensation insurance? In fact, most labor brokers considered these people independent contractors, even though many didn't meet the test that the IRS required for such a designation. The illegal immigrants they hired weren't paid by the hour, but by the job. If the job called for working nights or weekends, the money was the same. "Overtime pay" had no meaning in the shadow economy that increasingly supported the building trades.

This new economy grew largely out of sight. Most Americans weren't concerned about who was building their homes or offices. Illegal immigrants needed the work, the industry liked the cheap labor, and politicians called for stricter immigration policies but took no action.

As Stan watched these changes unfold, he became increasingly dismayed about the long-term sustainability of the construction business. On the one hand, fewer native-born Americans were going into construction. The business was no longer seen as a career, and more young people chose to pursue college degrees and jobs inside climate-controlled cubicle farms. Without the influx of Latino workers, legal or otherwise, the industry wouldn't have enough manpower to meet demand, even in slower economic times. But that manpower came at a price. Sure, the immigrants worked cheap, but their skills were entirely self-taught. Subcontractors didn't have the training programs that Marek had spent decades developing. Nor did they invest in their workers. They simply hired whoever they could find for a job. If someone got injured or complained, they were cast aside. Marek refused to change its policies, still investing in its workers, even though it often was underbid by competitors with lower labor costs.

In the name of cost, the construction industry was building an army of disposable workers, who remained hidden in the shadows of the economy.

If America's immigration policy didn't change, the construction business would face an unsustainable future: Work quality would decline as costs rose and workers—legal or illegal—became harder to find. Stan had spent years warning politicians, government bureaucrats, and his industry counterparts of the dangers. His entreaties were lost amid the industry's immediate, short-term fixation on cost and the anti-immigrant fervor that had taken hold in the country since 9/11. Simply put, whoever offered the lowest bid usually got the job, and Stan knew that by trying to do the right thing, he could be losing work.

The system wasn't working for anybody. It wasn't working for the immigrants, many of whom were exploited or abused by an arrangement in which they had little standing and no recourse if they were injured or denied pay. It wasn't working for the companies, which were in a race to the bottom—pursuing ever-lower wages while accepting poorer quality work. New recruits weren't trained, and they weren't protected. The system wasn't working for American society either: The U.S. was denied tax revenue from employees working off the books. States like Texas were overly burdened with the cost of illegal immigration even as their economies depended on the labor it provided.

Something had to change. The industry Stan had dedicated his life to was at stake. Stan knew that the ICE agents who had shown up in his lobby weren't going to go away, and they weren't going to fix the problem. Politicians were using immigration for political gain, but race-baiting and nationalism weren't solutions, he stressed. The situation required rational reform with cooperation from business owners like himself.

Immigration policy needed to reflect economic reality. Workers needed a stable environment through which they could participate in the economy without fear of deportation. That meant some sort of legal status. At the same time, the workers and their employers needed to pay their fair share. Stan might not be able to change the mindset of politicians, but he was determined to try. And while he was at it, he would strive to set an example for the rest of the construction industry.

2

The Two Percent Solution

For Stan Marek, immigration is the common thread that binds his past to the present and anchors the future. In 1882, his great-grandparents, Joseph and Anna Marek, emigrated to the United States from the Czech village of Olomouc, about one hundred sixty-five miles southeast of Prague. Joseph was a carpenter and Anna toiled in a cigar factory under appalling conditions that may have affected her health. Factory owners at the time exploited an abundance of unskilled labor, forcing people to work long hours seven days a week. Life was hard, and five of the couple's six children died at young ages.

The Habsburgs of Austria, who ruled what's now the Czech Republic, persecuted Czechs for their persistent nationalism, suppressing Czech culture and language and forcing many young men into military service. In the mid-1800s, the Austrian economy was deteriorating, and unemployment soared.[1] Joseph and Anna moved to other cities seeking work, but the rigid structure of their society, the lack of freedom and limited opportunities eventually convinced them to join a long line of people leaving the region for America. Many Germans in the 1830s and 1840s decided to start over in Texas, where land was abundant. Their Slavic neighbors—Bohemians, Moravians, Silesians, and Czechs—soon followed.[2] By the mid-1800s, seven hundred Czechs had settled in an area of Texas west of Houston and as far south as Victoria. By 1900, their numbers would swell to more than fifteen thousand.

Joseph and Anna boarded a ship to New York, then sailed for Galveston, a thriving city on the Texas coast. But the bustle of a port city, with its cotton exchange, rail yards, and maritime culture wasn't the lifestyle the Mareks wanted. They had had enough of the overcrowded city life back home. They wanted land where they could raise more children—their only surviving daughter, Caroline, came with them to America—and they wanted to be close to relatives who had already made the journey. They traveled by wagon one hundred sixty miles inland to Praha, a tiny hamlet between Houston and San Antonio.

Anna's sister and her family had settled there earlier among other Czech farmers. Joseph and Anna moved in with her for about six years before renting a farm in Yoakum, about forty miles away. Joseph worked for local farmers and within three years he'd saved enough money to buy land—one hundred fifty acres on a hill just west of town. Using the carpentry skills he learned in Europe, he built a large single-room house for the family. The Mareks would have six more children in Texas, and the entire family worked the farm, raising cotton, sugar cane, and corn.

The Mareks' good fortune in the New World didn't last. In 1899, Joseph died after his appendix ruptured, leaving Anna to run the farm and raise the children, four of whom were under the age of eleven. All of them worked the cotton fields. "You're not picking cotton," Anna told them, "you're picking money." Her youngest son, John Anton Marek, who was five years old, took his father's death hard. He felt an emptiness that spawned an intense insecurity. He refused to leave his mother's side, even to go to school, fearing that he would come home to find his mother dead, too.

When John Anton was nine, his mother finally insisted he attend classes. School made him miserable. He didn't like sharing unfamiliar surroundings with other children he didn't know. The teacher spoke English, which he couldn't understand because his family still spoke Czech at home. Nevertheless, he gave into his mother's demands and wound up attending school through eighth grade, the highest level offered at Yoakum's country school.

A year before he died, Joseph had bought a mule-driven press for making molasses from the sugar cane that he and other nearby farmers grew. With her husband gone, the press became Anna's financial savior. Farmers hauled their cane from miles away, often bringing their children, who played nearby during the pressing process. Among the children was a little girl named Hermina Peters, whose grandparents had emigrated from Austria in 1845. Hermina was the oldest of five children and had grown up on a two hundred-acre farm. Like the Marek children, she became proficient at picking cotton. Although she attended school, her mother—who was also named Anna, and who wrote serial fiction stories for two local Czech newspapers—augmented her daughter's education with lessons in music, geography, language, and mathematics at home. When Hermina turned fifteen, her mother sent her to a convent school in nearby Hallettsville.

As he grew, John Anton Marek overcame his insecurities and became an ambitious young man. He dreamed of having his own farm and admired the precision with which his mother managed the family's financial affairs. He decided he would plant twenty acres of cotton, share the profits with his mother and, if he did well enough, buy a new buggy with rubber tires, which was considered a status symbol in the farming communities of southeastern Texas.

John and Hermina had spent their childhood years playing around the cane press, but in the fall of 1916, when John was twenty-two, he noticed something different about her. Watching her run down the road, her locks of long, dark hair blowing in the wind, he thought she looked like an angel. "I had known Hermina all my life, but I never really noticed her before that day," he recalled years later. "Suddenly, I could not stop thinking about her." [3]

Every chance he got, John rode the family's old wooden-wheeled buggy over to Hermina's house, where they would sit and talk in the parlor. Twice a week, he brought her presents, but he still managed to save a hundred dollars. The cotton harvest brought in another fifty. He used the money to buy the buggy with the luxurious rubber tires he'd been dreaming about. He took Hermina for long rides in the country. One night they drove to a motion picture show in Shiner, another Czech community about eleven miles to the north. With Hermina's little sister, Milady, riding along as a chaperone, they saw D.W. Griffith's *The Birth of a Nation*. "It was a good movie, and we all enjoyed it," John said. [4]

Watching the film in the country theater in Shiner, John and Hermina had no idea that the movie's racist portrayal of African Americans and its celebration of the Ku Klux Klan would help spark a major shift in the country's immigration policy. The film contributed to fears that precipitated the first steps toward the criminalization of immigration that would frustrate John's grandson, Stan, a century later. But that evening, John wasn't ruminating on the movie. He had other thoughts on his mind.

– – – –

Even before America became America, the issue of how to welcome foreigners was controversial. The Founding Fathers wanted immigrants, but they wanted new arrivals who were farmers, craftsman, and artisans who could help build the fledgling country. They didn't want felons, debtors, and poor people following them across the Atlantic from Great Britain. Benjamin Franklin groused about the influx of Germans to Pennsylvania, finding them "the most ignorant stupid sort," while also decrying "all Blacks and Tawneys." [5,6] By the Nineteenth Century, unskilled workers were arriving from Poland, Italy, Ireland, and Portugal, adding to the friction with native-born Americans. The Massachusetts secretary of the commonwealth, in a report to the state legislature in 1857, declared that Irish immigrants were defined by their "wretchedness, beggary, drunkenness, deceit, lying, treachery, malice, [and] superstition." [7]

Although America had been happy for Chinese immigrants to come to the West Coast and help build the transcontinental railroad eastward, the Chinese weren't welcomed as potential citizens. To make that clear, Congress in 1882 passed the Chinese Exclusion Act, preventing Chinese nationals from becoming American citizens and essentially closing the door on all immigration from that country for decades. (In 1907, similar restrictions ended immigration from Japan.) Four years later, the Statue of Liberty was dedicated in New York Harbor. The statue faces southeast, welcoming the tired, poor and huddled masses yearning to breathe free that entered the harbor from the east, primarily Europe.

The second decade of the twentieth century was an optimistic time in America, despite the outbreak of war in Europe. Technological innovation seemed to arrive with each passing year—the opening of the Panama Canal, the expanding role of aviation, Henry Ford's creation of affordable automobiles. Theodore Roosevelt became the youngest president in the nation's history, and industrialization brought with it more leisure time. Movies emerged as a recreational craze across the country, and although farmers like the Mareks didn't have a lot of spare time, their children still flocked to the theaters on weekends.

Politically, the country entered the Progressive Era, a time of widespread activism and calls for reform. These new ideas clashed with the large groups of newcomers emigrating from southern and eastern Europe. These immigrants arrived much as the Mareks had, showing up at ports such as Galveston or, later, Ellis Island, which the federal government opened in 1892 adjacent to the Statue of Liberty. Today, people often refer to their ancestors coming to America "the right way," but there were no prior approvals or visas issued. In the 1800s, America essentially had no immigration policy. New arrivals were checked for communicable diseases and allowed to settle into the country. "Ellis Island was a quarantine station," said Charles Foster, the attorney who handled Marek's ICE audit. "The only requirement [for entry] was that you didn't have a contagious disease, or you weren't a criminal."

America's open borders were creating a demographic shift that concerned many whose ancestors had been in the country for a generation or more. Unlike previous immigrants from northern Europe, this new wave of Italians, Irish, Czechs, and others did not speak the English and German common in America at the time. And while America was predominately Protestant, many of these new immigrants were Catholics. Their arrival coincided with the rise of industrialization. Unlike the Mareks and others who came decades earlier and moved to farms scattered across the countryside, many newer immigrants worked in factories and settled in tenements in cities, where jobs abounded for skilled and unskilled workers alike. American lawmakers were confronted with a rising tide of social problems they hadn't experienced before—issues of assimilation, urban poverty and crime, and runaway population growth. By 1907, the U.S. had eighty-seven million people and more than a million immigrants were pouring into the country annually.[8] Progressives worried that unchecked immigration was inviting a host of "Old World" problems that would destabilize the country. But they were also confident that through careful study and reasoning, America could find a solution.

Today, the debate over immigration is split along partisan lines, but historically, both conservatives and liberals supported immigration restrictions for different reasons. Progressive thought at the time was dominated by "scientific research" that purported to show the superiority of some races—especially white, northern Europeans. In 1916, Madison Grant, a lawyer and zoologist, published *The Passing of the Great Race*, which gave rise to scientific racism. Grant divided the races into Caucasoids, Negroids, and Mongoloids, an idea he borrowed from the eugenics "science" of the nineteenth century.[9] His "research" found that Caucasoids were superior and the only race vital to human achievement.[10] He advocated using immigration policy to protect the American "stock" by restricting immigration from southern and eastern Europe. He also championed segregating "unfavorable" races into ghettos to prevent the Nordic, or northern European "race," from being diluted by undesirables [11].

Grant's book coincided with mounting fears about the Russian Revolution and the rising political influence of the Ku Klux Klan. Even before it was published, Grant's research was influencing members of Congress.[12] In 1907, the lawmakers empaneled the bipartisan United States Immigration Commission to study the origins and consequences of this new immigration wave. Led by William Paul Dillingham, a Republican senator from Vermont, the joint House-Senate group undertook a sweeping, comprehensive review. It operated on the belief that by categorizing and ranking groups based on their "desirability," ability to assimilate, and positive contributions to America, immigration-related problems could be solved through well-reasoned and methodical policies.

The commission's staff investigated the issue with intensity, studying how immigration affected every industry and all aspects of American life. Its agents, armed with questionnaires, interviewed thousands of workers in dozens of industries across the country, from shoemaking to banking. They categorized respondents by country of origin, literacy, property ownership, religion, criminal history, and character. Then, they contrasted the results with those of native-born Americans (many of whom were themselves children or grandchildren of immigrants). Agents even monitored and compared the academic performance of students in grade school. The commission's staff fanned out abroad, too, visiting most of the European nations from which recent immigrants came.

The effort took four years, and the results filled forty-one volumes. The investigators concluded that immigration from southern and eastern Europe posed a serious threat to American society and culture that should be restricted and reduced.[13] The report combined enthusiasm for the emerging ideas of eugenics as social science with growing xenophobia. It glorified immigration of the past while portraying "modern" immigration as something far more dangerous and harmful. Eugenics, once widely accepted as a "scientific" study of racial differences, was rejected by most true scientists of the day. Although it has since been widely debunked, its effects continue to influence modern discussions of immigration and racial equality. In 2018, for example, President Donald Trump, in rejecting a bipartisan immigration reform proposal pondered aloud why the U.S. should accept immigrants from "shithole" countries in Africa rather than nations such as Norway.[14] (By the 1930s, its popularity in the United States began to fade, but it caught the attention of Adolph Hitler as he rose to power in Germany. Hitler's *Mein Kampf*, published in 1925, praises America's policy of "simply excluding certain races from naturalization." Hitler also publicly lauded Madison Grant's *The Passing of the Great Race*, which had influenced America's exclusionary immigration policies.[15])

Most Americans didn't read the commission's full report, or even its executive summary. But the sentiments reflected in the Dillingham Commission's findings—that the country was being overrun by "undesirable" immigrants—began to take hold in popular opinion.[16] It was codified by the country's first blockbuster film—*The Birth of a Nation*. D.W. Griffith directed and produced the movie that John Marek and Hermina Peters saw in Shiner, Texas, in the fall of 1916. Released a year earlier, it was both a commercial success and a technological achievement in filmmaking. Griffith screened it for President Woodrow Wilson in the White House, the first time a motion picture was shown there. The three-hour silent film didn't address immigration directly. Instead, it focused on a threat that Griffith saw as more pressing—African Americans. The film portrayed blacks (many played by white actors in blackface) as stupid and dangerous, and the Ku Klux Klan as a heroic force taking a stand against society's destruction. Racial inaccuracies and injustices persist more than a century later. In the spring of 2020, the killing of a black man by a white police officer in Minnesota sparked protests that spanned the globe to condemn the brutality and inequality that African Americans still endure.

The Klan had been formed a year after the Civil War.[17] It went on to conduct a wave of violence and mayhem across the former Confederacy in the mid– to late 1800s. By the early twentieth century, though, the secret society had all but died out. The film, because of its wide distribution and commercial success, revived the Klan. More broadly, it recast the public's opinion of the group from a terrorist organization to noble defenders of Southerners facing the threat of the "black beast." [18]

On Thanksgiving 1915, William Joseph Simmons, a ne'er do well with a Jesus complex and a gift for self-promotion, led a group of men to the top of Stone Mountain, near Atlanta. They carried a Bible, an American flag, and a few planks of wood. When they reached the summit, they soaked the wood in kerosene and fashioned it into a giant cross, then set it ablaze. As the cross burned, they recited an "oath"—mostly made up words— as Knights of the Ku Klux Klan. Cross-burning hadn't been a part of the original Klan's rituals. Simmons took it directly from a scene in *The Birth of a Nation*.[19]

That gathering was small, and the group would grow slowly, but the event marked the beginning of the most powerful era in the racist organization's history. Building on what it termed the "science" of white superiority, the Klan expanded its racism to include foreigners as well as blacks. By the mid-1920s, the group had as many as four million members and wielded significant political influence, playing a role in electing nine Republican and seven Democratic senators and five Democratic governors. When Oklahoma Gov. John C. Watson attempted to curtail Klan activities, the group led a successful campaign to impeach him. It lobbied lawmakers to curb immigration and prevent the influx of "hereditary defectives" to the United States. Klan members inundated their representatives with petitions for anti-immigration laws.[20] The Klan's efforts, combined with congressional testimony from eugenicists who wanted to improve the human gene pool through selective breeding, inspired several restrictive laws. In 1917, Congress imposed a head tax and literacy test on new arrivals. In the early 1920s, the lawmakers curtailed immigration to 3 percent of each nationality already living in the United States. Immigration from southern and eastern Europe fell by almost five hundred thousand between 1920 and 1922. With the restrictions, the welcoming torch of the Statue of Liberty burned only intermittently, for those lucky enough to show up early in the month. The new laws allowed in so few southern Europeans that often a ship arriving on the first day of the month would fill the quota for the next thirty days. Ships coming in too late were turned away and left to steam back across the Atlantic. The race of immigrant-bearing ships became known as the "Immigrant Derby." Vessels would arrive early, then wait just outside the three-mile territorial boundary of U.S. waters on the last day of the month. Then, at the stroke of midnight, when the allowable number of immigrants reset, the ships would race toward shore.[21]

Congress implemented even more comprehensive restrictions in 1924. The National Origins Act capped at 2 percent each European nationality's population based on the 1890 Census and banned all immigration from Asia. The Klan used its influence to sway lawmakers, arguing that passing the law would reduce the number of Jews, Catholics, and other undesirables entering the country. Senator Ellison DuRant Smith, a South Carolina Democrat, echoed Madison Grant in his support for the law, arguing that America had "the largest percentage of pure, unadulterated Anglo-Saxon stock" and that the law would ensure "the preservation of that splendid stock."[22] Albert Johnson, a Republican from Washington who chaired the House Committee on Immigration and Naturalization, said the law amounted to "America's Second Declaration of Independence."[23]

Even though he opposed the Klan, President Calvin Coolidge signed the National Origins Act, stating that "America must remain American." It would limit immigration from all countries outside the Western Hemisphere to one hundred sixty-five thousand people a year—less than one-fifth the average arrivals prior to World War I.

For all its restrictions, the law didn't classify workers from Latin America, and Mexico in particular, as immigrants. They were considered a "temporary workforce" for American farmers—one that returned home at the end of the growing season. In fact, the restriction on Chinese labor left many growers in the West scrambling for field help and actually strengthened the demand for Mexicans.

By 1928, the Klan's influence was again waning. While the supremacist group would never return to the same mainstream stature that it enjoyed earlier in the decade, anti-immigrant sentiment would linger on and off over the next century. The National Origins Act implemented a policy that required immigrants to obtain a visa from an American consular office in their native country. Joseph and Anna Marek never faced such rules when they came to America four decades earlier. The visa program is still used today.

While the National Origins Act didn't specify racial restrictions on immigration, in practice it ensured that the racial and ethnic makeup of the country remained unchanged. If, for example, one thousand Greeks lived in the United States, then the law's "2 percent solution" limited Greek immigration to twenty. If, however, one hundred fifty thousand British immigrants were in the country, then three thousand more could come. Because the benchmark was tied to the immigrant populations of 1890, the law curtailed the influx of "undesirables." As Catholics from eastern Europe, the Mareks were lucky they fled their homeland as early as they did. Had they waited their descendants might never have made it to America.

The restrictions worked as intended. In 1925, immigration fell by more than 50 percent, with most of the migrants coming from Canada and Mexico. The number of Poles and Italians fell by an astonishing 90 percent.[24]

– – – –

Back in Yoakum, returning from *The Birth of a Nation* on that night in 1916, John Anton Marek could not have envisioned the turmoil immigration would spark in the U.S. over the next century. His thoughts of the future were more immediate. As they pulled up in front of Hermina's house, Hermina's sister went inside, giving the young couple some time alone. They held hands under the moonlight and talked about their dreams for the future. John said he wanted to start a farm and raise cotton and cattle. Hermina talked about the women in her life she respected, including her mother and two aunts who had become nuns. She admired how the pair had dedicated their lives to God, just like the Mother Superior at Hermina's convent school. She worried that she was spending too much time with John and neglecting her duties to God. "She had a faraway look that made my stomach sink," John recalled. "From the way she was talking, I could tell she was thinking of becoming a nun, too."

John didn't want to lose her and didn't have time to waste. Hermina was still explaining how important her religion was when John blurted out: "Hermina, I want you to marry me!" Any ideas she had about joining the convent were whisked away. Without a second thought, she said "yes." [25]

3

Help Wanted

As the "war to end all wars" ended, America emerged economically stronger and more assured of its dominance in the world. Wartime restraint gave way to peacetime excess, including jazz, flappers, and speakeasies of a nation ascendant. In 1927, Charles Lindbergh piloted his custom-built "Spirit of St. Louis" on the first trans-Atlantic flight, a testament to American ingenuity. Automobiles were whizzing off assembly lines in Detroit, making society more mobile. Radio broadcasts began unifying the country in a way it had never been connected before.

In Yoakum, the good times were more muted. John and Hermina made a living off the land, picking cotton and raising twenty-five acres of corn to feed the farm animals. By 1925, they had three boys—John Ladislaus Marek, the first born who was named after his father and nicknamed "Loddie;" William Albert, or Billie; and Rudolph Stanislaus, known as Ralph, who was born in 1925, one year after Coolidge signed the National Origins Act. The boys milked the cows twice a day and Hermina raised chickens and churned butter that she sold to other farmers.[1] John supplemented his income by blacksmithing for neighbors. Later, he branched into a thriving, if illicit, industry: moonshine. Prohibition outlawed liquor, but the corn that the Mareks produced on half their land fed John's still as well as his animals. Yoakum straddles Lavaca and DeWitt counties, midway between Houston and San Antonio, and John's recipe for corn whiskey was known throughout both regions. The Marek garage became a gathering place for neighbors. A county commissioner, who visited regularly, once even brought Texas Governor Dan Moody with him.[2] (Years earlier, Moody had gained fame as a district attorney for prosecuting Klansmen in the flogging of a man in Williamson County, north of Austin, whom they accused of committing adultery. The convictions Moody won marked the beginning of the end of the Klan's power in Texas.)

John and Hermina led a simple life. They managed the farm themselves without relying on migrant labor as some larger operations did. At the time, Mexican workers moved freely into Texas for planting and harvesting, finding work across the state, then returning home during the winter. To most Texans, the Mexicans weren't immigrants—they were cheap labor.

While World War I had halted most immigration from Europe, the U.S. Attorney General not only exempted Mexicans from the head tax and literacy tests required of immigrants, he actively recruited Mexican labor. The federal government imposed no limits on immigration from within the Western Hemisphere. In 1921, Congress capped total immigration at three hundred fifty-seven thousand, then gradually lowered the limit to one hundred fifty-four thousand by 1929 under the restrictions of the National Origins Act, but Mexicans continued to move freely across the border in large numbers.[3] As the Mexican Revolution escalated between 1913 and 1917, leading to the overthrow of the dictatorship (and eventually the creation of a constitutional republic), more Mexicans fled the violence and economic devastation to seek employment north of the border. By 1920, some two hundred thousand Mexicans had emigrated to the United States. That number would surge to three hundred thousand by 1930. Most had no intention of staying. They simply sought jobs that weren't available in Mexico at the time. As a result, economic interests on both sides of the border aligned to encourage the movement of this temporary workforce.

While the rest of the country was awash in nativism—Congress created the Border Patrol in 1924, the same year it passed the National Origins Act—the booming economy of the 1920s and the insatiable demand for unskilled labor trumped concerns about border security.[4]

For the Mareks, though, farming their fifty acres provided ample prosperity without any hired help. By 1927, they were doing well enough that John bought a Packard touring car, which he let Hermina drive. A year later, he bought a truck for himself. Yoakum didn't have many two-car families in those days, but John didn't stop there. He also bought a Fordson tractor and became one of the first mechanized farmers in the area. He learned how to repair it, and as other farmers also bought tractors, he expanded his blacksmithing business to include tractor repair.

He based his purchase on optimism that good harvests and strong cotton prices would remain steady. "We were well off, and I had very good credit with the bank," John recalled. "Rather than paying off my loans, the bank always encouraged me to put the money back into the farm."[5]

Even in good times, farming wasn't easy. In 1929, the average American earned seven hundred fifty dollars a year, while the average farmer earned just two hundred seventy-three— but only if the weather cooperated. With automation, farms became a victim of their own success. Tractors replaced horses and mules, and millions of acres that had grown feed became available for more cash crops. Farm production soared, outstripping demand. In an era before free trade, high import tariffs made U.S. farm exports uncompetitive in most other countries. By the end of the decade, American farmers were billions of dollars in debt.

The automation of farming coincided with a rise in manufacturing, which were both fed by skyrocketing consumption. More Americans began using credit to buy everything from radios to cars. On October 24, 1929, the stock market crashed, wiping out $30 billion of wealth in a matter of days and igniting a nationwide panic. Loan defaults increased, and nervous banks began calling notes. The Yoakum State Bank closed, and John and Hermina lost $500 in savings. Then, the Federal Land Bank demanded they repay their mortgage on the farm. They owed $1,275—far more than they could pay—and eventually the bank evicted the family from the home John had built.

For a while, the couple and their three boys—aged twelve, nine, and five—lived on part of the land owned by Hermina's parents. When Hermina's family, too, fell on hard times, her father had to sell the property. John and Hermina were forced to rent a dismal one-room house with a dirt floor in DeWitt County. The building had no indoor plumbing. A horse trough doubled as a bathtub, and light seeped through cracks in the siding.[6] "I never dreamed that I would bring my family to a place like that," John said later. "It was no more than a shack. The shame was almost more than I could bear."[7]

The desperate straits in which the Mareks found themselves were playing out across the country. As unemployment rose and the Depression deepened, more Americans became openly hostile toward Mexican immigrants. Thanks to the policies of the 1920s, European immigration was a shadow of what it had been. Without southern Europeans to blame, the public's ire shifted toward Mexican workers. They were now seen as responsible for the country's financial hardships and vanishing jobs and accused of mooching off welfare programs. Congress, unsure how to solve the country's economic crisis, responded to the public outcry by ordering federal troops to round up and deport thousands of Mexicans. Between 1929 and 1937, more than four hundred fifty-eight thousand were arrested and expelled from the country.[8] Resorting to force and police actions, and without regard for civil rights, Congress sought to correct its political indifference, which had allowed an influx of laborers from south of the border to flourish during the previous two decades. The about-face succeeded in curtailing Mexican immigration.[9]

– – – –

By 1935, Yoakum was caught in the teeth of both the Great Depression and a crippling drought. The first caused cattle prices to crater and the second dried up the grass to feed the animals. Through their mounting hardships, the Mareks had managed to hang onto ten malnourished cows. Desperate, the elder John Marek agreed to sell the animals to the government for five dollars apiece as part of a federal relief program for struggling farmers. The government didn't want to own cattle, but by reducing inventory it hoped to prop up prices. Federal agents came to the farm with a Caterpillar tractor, dug a ditch, and herded the cows into it. Then, using a high-powered rifle, they shot the animals one by one. Ralph, who was ten years old, watched in horror as the men slaughtered the cows he had milked that morning. Before they buried the carcasses, the agents allowed John to skin one of the animals, but the Mareks couldn't afford ice to preserve the meat. As young Ralph stared at the dead cattle in the ditch, the full magnitude of his family's hardship washed over him. "We had no cows, one horse, and we were living in a shack in sheer misery," he recalled some eighty years later. "It was by far the lowest point in our existence."[10]

John's dream of rebuilding his farm died with the livestock. "Those cattle were going to be our way out of poverty," he said. "I became very depressed. At night, I lay awake wondering where the money was going to come from to keep us alive. The future looked hopeless."[11] He turned to drink, consuming the whiskey he had made for others, and he descended into alcoholism.

Eventually, the family's luck improved. The owner of a farm in nearby Sweet Home invited the Mareks to stay there if John would rebuild the dilapidated farmhouse. John was a skilled carpenter, and he'd already built the house that he and Hermina had lived in when they got married. He jumped at the offer. At first, the move was worse than staying in their old shack. They had to live in the barn until John finished the house. With no new lumber available, he and the boys had to tear down the old farmhouse plank by plank and reuse the wood. It took several weeks, but they turned the pile of scrap lumber into a two-bedroom house surrounded by a white-picket fence.[12]

Slowly, the Mareks also rebuilt their lives. As the boys grew closer to adulthood, though, they could see that the Yoakum area offered few opportunities. Across the country, young people were leaving family farms and moving to cities, where incomes were steadier and amenities more abundant. One by one, John and Hermina's three sons made their way to the nearest big city, Houston.

– – – –

The first to leave was Loddie, the oldest son, who now wanted to be called "John L." By the time he was twenty-one, he was already handling most of his father's whiskey-making business, and he had no desire to continue scraping out a living as a tenant farmer like his dad. With fifty cents in his pocket, he hitched a ride to Houston and moved in with two aunts who ran a grocery. Unlike the sleepy farming town where John L. had grown up, Houston was an exciting metropolis teeming with three hundred eighty thousand people—the largest city in Texas. Through one of his aunts, he began an apprenticeship hanging gypsum wallboard, commonly known by the trade name Sheetrock.[13] The U.S. Gypsum Company invented wallboard, or drywall, in 1916 as an alternative to plaster. As the name implies, Sheetrock came in panels with powdery white gypsum sandwiched between sheets of heavy paper. The thickness varied between one-fourth and five-eighths of an inch. By the late 1930s, it was becoming a popular building material because it was lighter and cheaper than plaster, and less combustible than wood.[14] Sheetrock was easy to cut and hang, usually with nails to hold it to the wall studs. Once a piece of drywall was in place, the seams were taped and covered with a joint compound to create a smooth surface.[15] John's boss paid him twenty-five cents an hour, which even during the Depression was a paltry wage. But he managed to save some money and send some to his family in Yoakum. Drywall was cutting-edge building technology at the time, and demand grew steadily in the years leading up to World War II. John decided to go into business for himself. He met a Sheetrock salesman who alerted him to recent orders. Then, John contacted the builder and offered to install the material. He worked six days a week and hitched a ride home to Yoakum on Sundays. By 1939, he'd saved enough money to buy a three-year-old Ford sedan. A year later, his brother Bill, who'd been working for the Civilian Conservation Corps in Santa Fe, New Mexico, joined him in the business. A year after that, the youngest brother, Ralph, moved to Houston to be with the fledgling company.

Because Sheetrock was just coming into widespread use in the construction business, there were few experienced drywall installers. The brothers couldn't find enough skilled help to keep up with the orders. Still, the business did well enough that they built a new house and convinced their parents to move from Yoakum to Houston. Their father continued to drink heavily, beset by guilt at losing the family farm and, now, having to move into a house that his sons built for him.

When the Japanese bombed Pearl Harbor in December 1941, the American war effort halted most civilian construction. Many workers joined the service, and material was diverted to the war effort. The brothers shut down the business and enlisted. John and Ralph joined the Navy, and Bill became a mechanic in the Army Air Corps.[16]

– – – –

The Marek brothers exemplified a growing trend in the final years of the 1930s: the exodus from rural towns to burgeoning cities. As the effects of the Depression eased and industry ramped up production for the war, workers either enlisted, as the Marek brothers had, or gave up low-wage farm work for better pay in factories. As farm labor declined, a new concern arose: threats to the food supply. To ward off disruptions during wartime, the Roosevelt administration negotiated the Mexican Farm Labor Program Agreement in 1942. The program supplied American farmers with a steady stream of Mexican laborers known as *braceros*. The term was derived from *brazo*, the Spanish word for "arm" which can also be loosely translated as "manual laborer" or "farmhand." The Bracero Program guaranteed migrant farmworkers a minimum wage and humane conditions, including adequate shelter, food, and sanitation. Federal authorities delivered the first batch of some five hundred braceros to growers near Stockton, California, on September 29, 1942.[17]

During the next three years, the government recruited one hundred sixty-eight thousand braceros.[18] Envisioned as a temporary wartime workforce, most stayed after the war. As American agriculture expanded, with exports helping to feed war-ravished Europe, worries about labor shortages in the fields persisted.

Farmers lobbied Congress to extend the Bracero Program. Law-makers obliged, renewing the measure annually through the end of the decade.[19]

The initiative was popular especially in Texas because it created cover for undocumented workers. South Texas growers hired them off-the-books, continuing a cycle of exploitation of migrant workers that had been going on long before the Bracero Program began. In places like Starr County, non-Bracero migrants were paid as little as forty cents an hour to pick cantaloupes in the blazing sun, with no bathrooms or medical care. One worker described how he and his fellow migrants were given no water. He was forced to drink from bug-filled puddles left by the irrigation system.[20]

The braceros were supposed to leave at deadlines specified during their hiring. But they were earning higher wages and enjoyed better living standards than they had in Mexico, even if many lacked access to toilets and medical care. As many as two million stayed. Growers in Texas and elsewhere continued to hire them, either through the Bracero Program or independently. These overstaying braceros were the first real "undocumented workers," although growers faced no penalties for hiring them. In fact, the Texas delegation in Congress, under pressure from their state's farmers, passed the "Texas Proviso," which specifically exempted employers from prosecution for hiring undocumented Mexican workers. In 1949, the Immigration and Naturalization Service issued one hundred thousand temporary visas through the Bracero Program, but it wasn't enough to meet demand. A year later, the number of undocumented workers was estimated at eight hundred eighty-three thousand.[21] This disparity between the number of available visas and the demand for workers has only widened in the ensuing seventy years.

– – – –

John and Bill Marek were discharged from the service and returned to Houston to restart their drywall business in early 1946. They officially named it the Marek Brothers Sheetrock Installation Company. The Houston economy was booming. Oil output, curtailed during the war because steel was needed for weapons and military vehicles, came roaring back as petroleum producers raced to meet demand from a population embracing the automobile and moving to the suburbs. New subdivisions, combined with surging requests for retail space and office buildings, pumped hundreds of millions of dollars into the construction business.

The Mareks once again had more work than they could handle. Hermina, known to everyone as "Granny," joined the company to do the bookkeeping and answer the phones, but the brothers still couldn't find enough experienced drywall hangers. The Mareks expected crews to start at 5:00 a.m. and put in twelve- to fourteen-hour days, six days a week. That may have seemed like a normal workday on the farm, but most construction workers in Houston weren't interested in such rigorous shifts, especially for a physically demanding job hanging drywall in the heat and stifling humidity. The brothers found it easier to do the work themselves. The Mareks began to realize that city folks weren't cut out for the kind of grueling schedule the brothers had grown up with. Fortunately, they knew where to find a supply of like-minded workers: Yoakum. They decided to tap a labor pool where they knew people worked as hard as they did. Soon they were hiring extended family and friends and bringing them to Houston.

Ralph, meanwhile, was living in Corpus Christi, four hours down the Texas coast from Houston. He'd enrolled in the Navy in 1943 and had been stationed stateside. In Corpus, new recruits were immediately sent out in the hot Texas sun and taught how to march. On the second or third day, a voice came over the public address system asking if anyone knew how to hang Sheetrock. Ralph decided anything would be better than standing on the hot asphalt, and he had the required background, so he volunteered. The chief petty officers were building a club for themselves and the framing had been completed with prison labor. But they needed someone who knew how to hang drywall to train the prisoners. Ralph was their man.

The project didn't take long. Ralph didn't want to return to the boredom of marching, so he asked the head chief who would manage the new club. The chief said he hadn't given it much thought, so Ralph asked to be considered. He handed over a letter of recommendation from Earnest Coker, a restaurateur and family friend. The chiefs called a meeting and, after some deliberation, agreed to hire Ralph on a sixty-day trial. For the next two months he virtually lived in the club. At the end of the test period, no one doubted that Ralph was right for the job. He ran the club for the rest of his Navy career, scheduling entertainment, purchasing food, stocking liquor and supplies, organizing staff, and handling accounts. "That's when I learned about business," Ralph said.

Ralph put considerable energy into making the club profitable as well as a pleasant and entertaining place for chief petty officers to meet. He found a company in Corpus Christi, owned by a Mr. Henry, that rented juke boxes and slot machines and installed them in the club. Henry took 20 percent of the proceeds and the officers' club pocketed the rest. It was a lucrative agreement, and after about a year, Ralph decided to cut himself into the deal. He persuaded Henry to sell him the machines. He continued to pay the officers' club 80 percent of the takings, but now he kept the other 20 percent for himself. Ralph's cut turned out to be between two and three hundred dollars a month, a considerable sum at the time. Like his brothers, Ralph sent much of the money to his parents.

By keeping a tight control over the finances and the accounts, Ralph successfully put a stop to the usual pilfering associated with

Navy clubs. Most other officers' clubs lost money, but Ralph's generated a healthy profit.

As chiefs were discharged from the Navy, the club started to wind down and Ralph began looking for alternate employment. One day he was summoned to the officers' club, a lavish establishment on the base. It was a notch up from the chiefs' club, which was only for senior enlisted men. The commanding officer of the Naval Air Station told Ralph that he had reviewed the books at the chiefs' club and was so impressed with both the financial operations and social success of the establishment that he wanted Ralph to run the officers' facility. Ralph, who was barely twenty-one years old, was honored. He resigned from the chiefs' club and accepted his new position of general manager.

The officers and their wives not only had plenty of money to spend, they were also hungry for good food and fun. With a full staff of assistants and few restrictions, Ralph provided them with the entertainment and service they wanted. Ralph got the books under control, putting a stop to petty stealing, and the club started showing a profit. After several months, it was making enough money to attract top names like Russ Morgan, Harry James, and Alvino Ray. Big bands of this caliber cost as much as a thousand to fifteen hundred dollars a night.

In 1944, as Ralph was getting into the car he'd won in a poker game three days earlier to make a supply run into town, a Marine guard ordered him to drive two naval officers to the airport. Two nurses in full dress uniforms climbed into the back seat, and as Ralph drove, he couldn't stop staring at one of them. She was, he would say later "beauty personified." Ralph convinced the nurses to let him buy them a drink before their flight, and he managed to get the address of the one he was smitten with.

Martha Nolz was flying home to Zealand, North Dakota. Ralph wrote to her there, and they struck up a courtship when she returned to the base. The relationship violated Navy rules because

Martha was an officer, and officers weren't supposed to fraternize with enlisted men. By August 1945, they decided to get married, and Ralph convinced a group of nuns at a local hospital to stage a clandestine ceremony in the chapel. The couple said their wedding vows at 5:30 a.m. so that Martha could report for duty at 8:00 a.m.

Despite the need to keep their marriage secret, life was good. Ralph's job paid well, and he bought a three-bedroom house in a pleasant subdivision. But the demands of running the club meant Ralph spent little time at home. He seldom got in before 2:00 or 3:00 a.m. and was back at work soon after daybreak. Martha took an increasingly dim view of the situation, particularly after the birth of their first son, Stan, in 1947. Eventually, with the war over and officers receiving their discharges, attendance at the club declined. Ralph found that running the club was no longer the challenge that it had been, and he resigned.

Ralph wasn't sure what he would do. He'd been selling life insurance on the side while in the Navy, and he considered going into the business full time. Salesmanship came easily to him, but he didn't like pressuring people to buy something, and the thought of selling insurance for the rest of his life was unappealing.

His brothers had been writing to him about the housing shortage in Houston, which was driving demand for construction. They believed the city was on the cusp of unprecedented growth, and they could use Ralph's help. Leaving Corpus meant Ralph and Martha would have to sell the home that they loved and accept a lower standard of living, at least at first. With no place to live, they would have to move in with Ralph's parents. Ralph decided it was worth the inconvenience, and on the first day of 1948, they loaded young Stan in the car and headed for Houston. Martha cried the whole way.

Of the three brothers, Ralph was the only one who'd graduated from high school, and his experience with the officer clubs had taught him the basics of accounting and business management.[22]

His brothers desperately needed his help. The day after the family arrived in Houston, Ralph showed up at the Marek Brothers' office, ready to rejoin the family business.[23]

4

Immigration Becomes Illegal

Ralph's financial acumen made him a natural to lead the business. Even though Ralph was the youngest, his brothers, John L. and Bill, put him in charge. The new boss quickly found himself battling a perpetual labor shortage because of the company's growth and the physical demands of the job. "The turnover was unbelievable," Ralph recalled. "For every twenty men we would hire, we were lucky to get one to stay. I spent a lot of time trying to salvage men, because I figured if we invested the time in training them, we should try to keep them on."[1]

Hard work was engrained in the fabric of immigrant communities like Yoakum. The town's founding families and their children worked harder because they had to overcome greater adversity, arriving with little money, scratching out a life in the harsh Texas climate, and then enduring the Depression. At the rate the Mareks' drywall business was growing, though, hiring friends from Yoakum and surrounding communities wasn't enough to sustain the company. Ralph believed there was a better way to build the business. In the 1950s, construction had a reputation for overworking laborers and caring little about their well-being. Tradesmen had no paid vacations or job security and few benefits. If they were injured and couldn't work, they lost their jobs. Ralph found this situation callous and short-sighted. Ralph believed that by treating workers better, the Mareks would attract and retain higher-caliber employees. He initiated a policy of paying his team above the average hourly rate. As a result, the company's prices were 5 percent to 10 percent higher than its competitors. This put it at a disadvantage during the post-war building boom. To offset customers' price concerns, Marek Brothers emphasized quality work and customer service to distinguish it from lower-cost rivals. The brothers gave their employees regular raises and promotions, Christmas bonuses, and paid vacations. They also instituted a program to train workers in their craft, a benefit that was unheard of in the industry at the time.[2] Ralph focused on morale, too. Because of the heat during long workdays, the company set up a recreation lounge where employees could have a cold beer and shoot pool after their shifts. Ralph cosigned on workers' car loans and later offered a program to build them homes and secure discounted mortgages.

By the end of the decade, Marek Brothers had seventy employees. The business was generating so much cash that Ralph and his brothers began looking for ways to invest the excess profit. Certificates of deposit were paying less than 4 percent—below the inflation rate—and Ralph didn't trust the market for stocks and bonds. For a while, the brothers bought gold with their profits and buried it in their backyards. Rising inflation was driving up home prices, and in 1956, the men found a better use for their money. They formed a subsidiary, Stanley Construction, named after Ralph's oldest son, to capitalize on the suburban housing boom. Stanley built homes on land the brothers bought on Blue Bell Road in what was then the northern reaches of Houston. The company completed about two homes a month. The houses sold as soon as they were built—often to Marek employees, who received low financing rates from the company. Over the next twenty years, Blue Bell Village would expand to more than eighty acres.[3]

– – – –

The Mareks' practice of treating their workers better than most construction companies in Houston set the brothers apart and eased the company's labor shortage.[4] The city's construction business in the 1950s didn't rely on Mexican labor. Instead, European immigrants — Czechs, like the Mareks, as well as workers of German and Irish descent— dominated the industry. In the fields of south Texas, it was a different story. The demand for vegetable pickers and other farm laborers continued to grow unabated, at odds with immigration policy. At the same time, the U.S. economy slipped into recession, prompting a new wave of complaints that immigrants were taking American jobs— one of the oldest criticisms of immigration. Even though this gripe has remained popular for more than a century, there's almost no economic research that gives the notion credence.

Lawmakers embraced the same two-pronged strategy that presidents and other leaders would invoke in coming decades: Strengthen the border to keep out new entrants and create a legal status for those undocumented workers already in the country.[5] The rising paranoia sparked by the Red Scare and McCarthyism conflated illegal immigration concerns with fears about national security[6] and communist infiltration.

Some congressmen, however, saw a link between immigration and foreign policy. Emanuel Celler, a Democratic representative from New York, believed the quota system enacted in 1924 was too restrictive. By favoring immigration from northern and western Europe, the policy was creating resentment toward the U.S.

in other parts of the world, particularly eastern Europe and Asia, where communism was on the rise. In contrast, two other Democrats, Pat McCarran of Nevada and Francis Walter of Pennsylvania, worried that loosening the restrictions would make the country more vulnerable to infiltration by communists who would undermine the American way of life. McCarran and Walter proposed a law that would, among other restrictions, essentially bar all Asians and most Jews from entering the country. McCarran associated both groups with communism. "We have in the United States today hard-core, indigestible blocs which have not become integrated into the American way of life, but which, on the contrary, are its deadly enemies," he said. "Today, as never before, untold millions are storming our gates for admission, and those gates are cracking under the strain."[7]

In 1952, Congress approved the McCarran-Walter Act, which reinforced the immigration quotas adopted almost thirty years earlier. Progressives opposed it, and President Harry Truman vetoed it, calling it un-American and discriminatory. He argued that the isolationist policies that had been invoked in the 1920s would now play into communist hands. "We do not need to be protected against immigrants from these countries," Truman said in issuing his veto. "On the contrary, we want to stretch out a helping hand, to save those who have managed to flee into Western Europe, to succor those who are brave enough to escape from barbarism, to welcome and restore them against the day when their countries will, as we hope, be free again....These are only a few examples of the absurdity, the cruelty of carrying over into this year of 1952 the isolationist limitations of our 1924 law."

Congress overrode his veto, but to diminish the law's impact, Truman empaneled the President's Commission on Immigration and Naturalization, which issued reports criticizing the quota system. In 1954, two years after the veto override, the Immigration and Naturalization Service came up with a compromise that calmed the fears of nativists and lawmakers while addressing the labor concerns of the agricultural industry. The INS stepped up arrests of undocumented workers while at the same time expanding the total number of visas issued under the Bracero Program to four hundred fifty thousand.

In a program officially known as Operation Wetback, Border Patrol agents swept through the fields of California, Arizona, and Texas, arresting more than a million illegal immigrants and deporting them. It was the largest mass deportation in American history. The dragnet also ensnared legal citizens of Mexican ancestry, fostering an environment of fear that caused many Mexican workers to leave voluntarily.[8] Ironically, the program also gave legal status to many of the same workers who were deported. In numerous cases, the Border Patrol handed the detainees off to Labor Department agents waiting at the border who processed the workers, granted them visas under the Bracero Program, and returned them to the very fields from which they'd been arrested. Operation Wetback created the appearance of a crackdown on border security, while basically legalizing thousands of workers who'd been in the country illegally.[9]

Over the next six years, the program dramatically reduced the number of undocumented Mexican workers, from thirty-seven per thousand in 1954 to about one per thousand in 1960. In effect, Operation Wetback extended the success of the Bracero Program. During its twenty-two years, some five million Mexicans emigrated to the United States under the program.[10]

The Bracero Program fundamentally changed U.S. labor markets by giving Mexican workers a near-monopoly in agricultural labor. By the mid-1960s, American growers had become dependent on these laborers and their low wages to keep food prices down. For their part, the Mexicans grew accustomed to life in America. Many stayed in the country rather than returning home after the growing season.[11]

Truman's successors, Dwight Eisenhower and John F. Kennedy, condemned the quota system of immigration law. By the 1960s, the public came to see U.S. immigration policies as antiquated and even racist. The burgeoning civil rights movement and a change in sentiment that viewed foreigners more positively fueled mounting calls for immigration reform. Civil rights protests dovetailed with the farm worker movement. The Bracero Program may have encouraged the influx of Mexican workers, but it did little to protect them from low wages, and often deplorable living conditions. Congress terminated the program in 1964, but the change had little practical impact. Mexican workers continued to cross the border, just as they always had, to take jobs in the fields. Now, they were crossing the border illegally, but no one seemed to notice.

For all of politicians' focus on civil rights and immigration, the issue of Mexican workers captured little of their attention. The nation's leaders were more concerned with ending the quota system that had defined immigration law for four decades. In his 1964 State of the Union address, President Lyndon B. Johnson told Congress: "We must also lift by legislation the bars of discrimination against those who seek entry into our country, particularly those who have much needed skills and those joining their families. In establishing preferences, a nation that was built by the immigrants of all lands can ask those who now seek admission: 'What can you do for our country?' But we should not be asking: 'In what country were you born?'" [12]

In October 1965, Johnson signed the Immigration and Nationality Act in a ceremony at the base of the Statue of Liberty. Officially known as the Hart-Celler Act, the measure abolished consideration of national origin, race, religion, or ancestry as a basis for entry. Instead, it created seven categories, giving priority to relatives of American citizens, legal permanent residents, professionals and "special" immigrants such as clergy, foreign employees of the U.S. government, and graduate students. By signing the bill into law, Johnson ended the quota systems that had long favored people from northern and western Europe. Between 1492 and 1965, Europe accounted for 82 percent of all immigrants to America, a study by the Kinder Institute for Urban Research at Rice University found. After 1965, 88 percent came from countries outside of Europe.[13]

With the end of the Bracero Program, Mexicans technically now would be treated as any other immigrant group under the law. This shift toward equality in immigration policy unintentionally gave birth to the modern concept of illegal immigration. Previous laws had largely ignored numerical limits on immigrants within the Western Hemisphere. The 1965 law, however, ended the long-standing practice of considering Mexicans and other Latin American migrants to be temporary workers. It imposed a cap of one hundred twenty thousand immigrants not just from Mexico, but from the entire Western Hemisphere, which included Canada, Mexico, Latin and South America, and the Caribbean.[14] Yet between 1960 and 1968, the final year before the numerical restrictions took effect, Mexicans had received more than three hundred eight-six thousand permanent resident visas from the U.S. State Department. In other words, the influx of Mexicans at the time Johnson signed the law already exceeded the caps that the new measure imposed on all Latin America and Canada.[15]

For the Mexican workers who wanted jobs, the new law initially didn't change much. They continued to cross the border with few restrictions, and U.S. employers looking for cheap labor continued to hire them. Charles Foster, Stan Marek's immigration attorney, remembers working odd jobs as a teenager in McAllen, Texas, side by side with Mexicans who were technically in the country illegally. The border remained a relatively fluid place, with Mexicans crossing into the U.S. and Americans wading across the Rio Grande for hunting trips or to go bar hopping in border towns.

Mexican workers grew accustomed to living in America and didn't return home like they once did. Instead, they settled in the U.S. without immigration papers—disregarding the new law either deliberately or unknowingly. From the moment it was signed, the 1965 law ignored the economic issues driving the influx of Mexican labor and set the stage for criminalizing immigration on an unprecedented scale.[16]

– – – –

Political upheaval, rapid population growth, and a slowing economy in Mexico sparked a surge in immigration to the United States. But Mexicans now found themselves competing for a limited number of visas with Cuban refugees. Because of the U.S. government's anti-Castro policies, Cubans received priority for visas. A group of Mexican plaintiffs ultimately sued the Immigration and Naturalization Service and won. In 1977, a federal court would order that the State Department reassign one hundred forty-five thousand visas designated for Cuban refugees to Mexican immigrants in addition to the hemispheric caps the law imposed.

As the 1970s dawned, immigration began to rise after decades of decline as the 1965 reforms opened the United States to new immigrants, especially from Asia. More of these new immigrants were non-white than at any time in American history. In 1960, seven of eight immigrants were white Europeans. By 2010, the ratio would plummet to less than one in ten.[17] The increase in non-white immigration, though, coincided with a slowing U.S. economy in the 1970s. The nation was battered by soaring gasoline prices, stagnant wage growth, rising unemployment, and runaway inflation. As in previous decades when the American economy struggled, the country blamed immigrants. Beginning in 1976, Congress tightened immigration laws yet again. First, lawmakers stipulated that American-born children couldn't sponsor their parents for citizenship unless the child was at least twenty-one years old. Then, Congress eliminated the hemispheric limits altogether and set a worldwide cap of two hundred ninety thousand visas annually, which it reduced in 1980 to two hundred seventy thousand.

With the end of the Bracero program, Mexicans continued arriving in the United States seeking economic opportunity, but now they were classified as illegal immigrants. Between 1965 and 1986, an estimated twenty-eight million Mexicans crossed the border illegally, compared with 1.3 million who immigrated legally.[18] For those who wanted to enter the country "the right way," there simply wasn't a mechanism to accommodate so many people, even if they had jobs in the U.S. Immigration law had become completely untethered from reality.

5

A New Era of Mexican Labor

Stan Marek knew little of the changes to immigration law or what they would mean for the construction business when he graduated from Texas A&M University in 1969. After six months' active duty in the Marine Corps, he joined the family business in 1970 and became a union drywall mechanic with Carpenters Local 213. He had spent part of every summer since he was twelve years old working for his father's company.

By the 1960s, Houston had become the sixth-largest city in America. It had long been a hub for trade, since the first shipment of West Texas cotton left its port for foreign markets in 1919. Along the fifty-mile stretch of the Houston Ship Channel, which runs from Galveston Bay, up the San Jacinto River to a terminus four miles east of downtown, refineries and chemical plants sprang up, supplying energy and raw materials to the world[1]. The city was ideally situated between onshore oil drilling sites in the interior of the state and the Gulf of Mexico, where offshore drilling was pushing the boundaries of energy technology. Houston became home to the National Aeronautics and Space Administration's Mission Control. By the end of the decade, the city's name would become one of the first words spoken on the moon. The decade also saw the construction of the world's first indoor stadium, the Houston Astrodome. With its soaring, eighteen-story ceiling and massive air-conditioned interior capable of housing more than forty-two thousand people, it was one of the most audacious public works projects of the decade. When the futuristic stadium opened in April 1965, some hailed it as the Eighth Wonder of the World. The city's Major League Baseball team changed its name from the Colt 45s to the Astros, a nod to NASA's presence. Earning the nickname Space City, USA, Houston was the essence of modern, post-war American urbanism – bold, optimistic, and forward-looking

Marek Brothers benefited from the city's image, and the building boom that went with it. The company was handling about 20 percent of the all the drywall business in town. Houston's rapid expansion contributed to Marek's annual growth rate of 10 percent to 15 percent. Just as residential building had surged in the 1950s, commercial office building would dominate the 1960s. The Mareks positioned their company to capture the enthusiasm.

The breakneck growth presented a challenge for the firm. During most of the decade, Marek Brothers fought to retain its workers amid mounting competition. Customers balked at paying more for the Mareks' expertise, despite the higher quality. Workers, meanwhile, would defect to competitors for a few cents more an hour—and they didn't seem to care about the health and retirement benefits that Marek Brothers offered. The company wrestled with labor shortages as it tried to keep pace with Houston's real estate boom. As the nation's energy capital, the city was largely insulated from the oil shocks that roiled the economy in other parts of the country during the 1970s. Soaring oil prices kept the city growing and drew tens of thousands of middle-class workers fleeing the economic decline of northern cities. Marek began getting contracts outside of Houston. It expanded to Austin, San Antonio, and other Texas cities while starting to take on larger and more complicated jobs.

When Stan stepped into the family business in 1970, he found a company whose growth mirrored Houston's own economic surge. But despite the commercial construction boom, Marek still focused on residential drywall projects. A developer approached the company about the finishing work for a movie theater, and the brothers realized that commercial jobs were a huge untapped market. They set up a commercial division, which required them to accept a union for the first time.

The Mareks' residential business had always been an "open shop." Although Texas wasn't a stronghold for unionized labor, most commercial construction companies were unionized. The Mareks didn't buck the trend. For Ralph, working with labor groups wasn't difficult because he was already paying most of his workers above-market rates and offering benefits that many competitors didn't. Despite the tight job market, he prided himself on his workers' long tenures. Many had been with the company their whole careers. Ralph's credo for business was simple: Happy workers do better work. "We didn't sell on price; we sold on quality," he said. He insisted on offering good pay and benefits because of his own struggles early in life. "I always wanted to be someone who took care of my employees because I was so damn poor myself" growing up, he said.[2] He wanted to ensure that his own workers had the means to provide for their families in a way that his own father never could.

Marek employees enjoyed perks beyond their paychecks. Both union and non-union workers could get payroll advances at no interest, and Ralph frequently cosigned on loans for them. When Ralph was in his eighties, and no longer involved in daily operations, he took the distributions from his retirement account to set up a mortgage company for employees to buy homes at discounted interest rates. He added to the portfolio over the past decade and it was worth some three million dollars by 2016. "He's always told me, 'Stan, I came into this world with nothing. I'm going to leave with nothing,'" Stan recalled. Ralph died in April 2020 at the age of 95.

With the building boom, the industry experienced a subtle economic shift. Skilled workers who were employed by residential homebuilders began filling the higher-paying commercial jobs. Mexican laborers stepped into the jobs these men left behind in homebuilding. Many of the new arrivals worked hard and were good employees—and they were willing to work for less money, a boon to homebuilders' profit margins. Those who didn't speak English or didn't have legal status under the 1965 Immigration and Naturalization Act often found work with labor subcontractors. Established drywall companies would then hire the subcontractors, with their workforce of immigrant labor, on a piecework basis.

By the end of the 1970s, Marek's drywall business was the biggest in Houston. Most of its fifty-eight competitors had resorted to contract labor. This allowed them to avoid payroll taxes and save on benefits, overtime pay, and other expenses. The pressure on Marek to use "subs" intensified. In the 1960s, small companies did most of the homebuilding. But a decade later, large national conglomerates dominated the residential building market. They wanted work done at the lowest possible price, and often relied on subcontractors.

During this shift Stan was being groomed to take over the entire company from his father. He was still working for the commercial division and, isolated from the changes in the residential business, he didn't appreciate the extent to which the transformation in the labor force and hiring practices would come together to threaten the entire industry. Ralph and his brothers hoped their children would join the company. After all, Stan and his cousins knew the business from the ground up, having helped out by sweeping floors and picking up nails around the office when they were in elementary school. Stan had spent summers in high school hanging drywall and learning carpentry.

Everyone at the company knew Stan would be the boss one day. Even so, he didn't have an easy transition. Stan and Ralph had a distant relationship. Ralph was dedicated to running the company. He rarely spent time with Stan and his brother, Tommy, as they grew up. Ralph attended few of his sons' high school baseball, basketball, and football games. Stan recalls his dad visiting campus only once in his four years at Texas A&M. When Stan graduated from Marine Corps boot camp, Ralph was one of the few parents who didn't attend the ceremony. Ralph simply didn't feel he could take his eye off the company. His brothers and entire extended family were counting on him. Even though the business was thriving, Ralph lived with a constant fear of failure, worrying that the good times wouldn't last. "He was trying to make up for everything he had experienced during the Depression in his childhood—losing everything, his father becoming an alcoholic," Stan recalled. "I know Dad and his brothers grew up with a lot of fear, watching their dad drinking more and more, watching their cattle slaughtered by the government. He always made us feel like we were on the brink of bankruptcy."

Stan's full-time entry into the company would begin a years-long process of mending the relationship with his father. (At the time of Ralph's death, the two were quite close.) In an interview in 2017, Ralph called Stan a good son, and Stan admired his father. Stan's first two years as a union carpenter hanging drywall on office buildings gave him a taste of the hard work the company expected. And, much like Ralph, Stan developed empathy for those who did the work. "My dad has always been very cognizant of what it's like to go out there eight hours a day and bust your tail, getting dirty and being looked down on by people when you're at the construction site," Stan said. "My dad always modeled the conviction that you've got to take care of your people." [3]

– – – –

In the decade after the 1965 reforms broadened the scope of U.S. immigration policy, Mexican laborers entered a sort of round rob-in of deportation. Border Patrol agents were rewarded for appre-hending as many illegal immigrants as possible and processing their deportations quickly. The immigrants, once arrested, *wanted* to be deported quickly, so they could slip back across the border and return to work. Almost all immigrants ensnared by the Bor-der Patrol signed "voluntary departure orders" stipulating that they waived their rights to a hearing and agreed to return to Mex-ico—only to start the process of crossing back again immediately. "The border is a revolving door...," the U.S. comptroller general wrote in a 1976 report. "We repatriate undocumented workers on a massive scale...[and] the illegals cooperate by agreeing to volun-tarily depart, and significant numbers promptly re-enter." [4]

The number of deportations and growing Latino communities in large American cities made illegal immigrants—or at least the issue of illegal immigration—more visible. By the late 1970s, U.S. economic turmoil caused by the "stagflation" of high interest rates, high unemployment, and weak growth created anxiety that dovetailed with rising concerns that Mexican labor was prolifer-ating and taking jobs from out-of-work Americans. Lawmakers responded by introducing bills in the early 1980s designed to curb illegal immigration. [5]

During the previous five decades, Mexican workers had become a fixture of the Texas labor markets. Amid the economic hard-ships of the 1970s, many moved from the fields of South Texas to the cities, where they found homebuilding jobs. Cash-strapped builders were happy for laborers willing to work for less money, and construction companies or their subcontractors snapped them up. Later, many of the subcontractors would themselves be illegal immigrants—creating a system in which subs exploited other subs, all hidden in the economic shadows.

Marek didn't like the new piecework system of homebuilding that was emerging. The company had spent decades developing what it considered a good relationship with its employees by providing benefits and training. Ralph Marek had long advocated a "cradle-to-grave" approach to worker relations. He believed companies should take care of employees for their entire lives, in hopes that lifelong employment would encourage loyalty, better quality for customers, and strong financial results for his firm. But increasingly, Marek's competitors were focusing on the short-term. This affected more than the companies: It spilled over into the unions. In commercial drywall, which was more complicated than residential work and required special training, Marek employees were unionized. In the homebuilding division, they weren't. By the late 1970s, unions were losing some of their clout in the workplace, and the Mareks worried that the piecework practices of the residential industry would creep into commercial construction as well.[6]

As union power waned toward the end of the decade, Congress took steps that expanded the role of contract workers. In 1978, lawmakers amended the federal tax code to allow businesses to classify contract workers as "non-employees." This meant employers didn't have to withhold federal taxes or pay benefits. They simply hired the labor for a specific job and let the workers worry about their own health care, retirement, and taxes. Workers were essentially self-employed. Previously, companies avoided hiring independent contractors because the Internal Revenue Service often would retroactively reclassify them as full-time employees and require the companies that hired them to pay taxes and benefits later. Businesses complained that the Internal Revenue Service was too aggressive in its reclassifications. The changes in the tax code created a "safe harbor" for employers, who now felt freer to consistently treat employees as independent contractors.

While the rule was designed to protect employers who acted in good faith and were hiring contractors legitimately, in reality, it allowed many companies to classify workers as contractors for tax purposes even when they were full-time employees. It's not hard to see why employers were attracted to this ploy: Misclassification saved them 20 percent or more on labor costs because they weren't paying federal payroll taxes.

Employers at first were careful to make sure everyone working for them actually signed contracts and received 1099 tax forms that report miscellaneous income paid to nonemployees. "Once it became clear that there was this whole new workforce where you didn't really have to worry about the niceties of this kind of system, the system shifted from misclassification to just under-the-table, off-the-books cash compensation," said Mark Erlich, a fellow at the Harvard Labor and Worklife Program. Increasingly, workers were simply told they were being reclassified.[7]

Employers who abused the system, especially in the construction industry, could exploit desperate or migratory workers by denying them benefits and often not paying overtime or workers' compensation. Even if employers were caught misclassifying their workers as non-employees, the law prevented retroactive enforcement, which meant they didn't have to pay back taxes.

Misclassification would become a major issue in the construction business in the three decades after Congress changed the tax code. The new tax rules made it easier to hire illegal immigrants by designating them as independent contractors. By 2016, misclassification in Texas alone was estimated to top $1.2 billion in lost federal tax revenue annually. Nationwide, the number was about $17 billion in 2019, and some two million workers were affected, Erlich said.

Stan would learn the full effect of worker misclassification over the next decades. As he was promoted to president of Marek Brothers in April 1982, the changes in both immigration and tax policy were ushering in a new type of construction workforce—one that was less skilled and worked off the books, with little accountability. The change embodied the heart of the labor inequities that Stan would fight to rectify.

– – – –

Stan ascended to the top of the company at a terrible time. The Texas economy was on the verge of collapse, although few realized it then. To encourage domestic oil production after the 1979 Iranian oil embargo sent prices soaring, President Jimmy Carter deregulated oil prices. Crude shot from less than $16 a barrel in 1980 to almost $40 at the end of the next year. By 1985, the U.S. boosted domestic oil production by almost 420,000 barrels a day. The boom played well in Houston, where some of the city's biggest employers filled their coffers with newfound oil wealth. But as often happens in the oil business, success gave way to glut, and prices plunged. By 1986, a barrel of oil was selling for less than $10, devastating the Texas economy. Prices wouldn't recover for a decade. In Houston, one out of every seven workers lost their jobs. Real estate values plunged. Banks, many of which were overextended on loans to the energy and construction industries, failed at an alarming rate. By 1989, nine of the state's ten biggest banks had collapsed. Houston—like other Texas cities—found itself awash in unused office space.

The downturn hit Marek hard. Construction work dried up almost overnight. The company's revenue slowed to a trickle, making it difficult to fund operations and cover debt. "We had borrowed a lot of money from the bank in our normal course of doing business," Stan said. The company also had continued in-

vesting in its Blue Bell Village development, building rental houses and duplexes in north Houston. With the crash, Marek lacked
the liquidity to meet the requirements of its bonding company.
Then, Marek's lender failed, like hundreds of other banks across
the state. The government's Resolution Trust Corporation took
over the bank. While the move didn't pose a risk to depositors,
the RTC tightened lending requirements just when businesses
like Marek Brothers needed more credit.

Although Ralph was no longer running the daily operations,
he continued to oversee the business as chairman. The crisis required all of his financial savvy to keep the company afloat. He
converted short-term debt to long-term debt and mortgaged real
estate that the company had owned free and clear for years. Ralph
had seen his own father wiped out by debts of less than two thousand dollars. The fear of failure that had kept Ralph at the office
so many nights and weekends when Stan was growing up now
seemed justified. He almost lost the company he and his brothers
had built over forty years.

As the oil bust worsened, maintaining the generous benefits for
which Marek Brothers was known became a struggle, especially
in the company's unionized commercial shop. When Stan joined
as a union carpenter in the 1970s, the arrangement was simple:
Employers paid an hourly wage, overtime, and benefits, as stipulated by federal wage and hour laws. In return, workers earned a
solid middle-class income. But across the country, shifting economics had been reshaping the American workforce, especially in
the building trades.

U.S. union membership peaked at twenty million members in
1979.[8] It has fallen ever since. While the reasons for the decline
are many, two key factors stand out: the failure of the Labor Reform Act of 1978 to safeguard union power and President Ronald
Reagan's firing of more than eleven thousand striking federal air
traffic controllers in 1981. The reform legislation sought to remove

obstacles to union elections and enable workers to unionize more easily. The proposal failed, despite Democratic control of the U.S. House of Representatives and support from the Carter administration, after an effort by sympathetic senators came two votes shy of overriding a Republican filibuster. The defeat marked the end of union power that had arrived with the New Deal.[9] Reagan's firing of the air controllers ushered in a new anti-union sentiment that would take hold across the country in the 1980s.

In Houston, Marek continued to pay union wages, but it increasingly found itself losing business to proliferating non-union competitors. As union power waned, the company struggled to find workers. Yet Marek soon discovered a labor pool eager to join the industry ranks: Mexican immigrants.

– – – –

As the 1980s wore on, it became clear that it was time for the next generation of Mareks to take over the company. Ralph's brothers, John L. and Bill, were no longer involved in daily operations, and in 1988 Ralph relinquished his chairman's title to Stan. John L.'s two sons, Bruce and Paul, joined him as partners. This new batch of Mareks found themselves leading a company in an industry that was unlike the one their fathers had known. The economic malaise had become a full-scale recession, which hit the construction and real estate markets hard. "The three brothers, they had basically made enough money to pay off all our debt and everything, and then here's the second generation, and it starts losing money," Bruce Marek said. "It was definitely a humbling experience."

The recession changed the nature of the workforce. As construction demand declined and union membership faded, companies looked for the cheapest labor source to squeeze as much profit as they could from meager sources of revenue. For most of the decade, the number of Latino workers in construction continued to grow. Because most of these laborers worked for lower wages, few employers questioned their immigration status. By 1986, undocumented workers in the U.S. topped four million, as attempts to crack down on illegal border crossings failed.

Social organizations began to question the treatment of immigrant workers, expressing concerns that resonated with the public. In response, Congress passed the Immigration Reform and Control Act, which provided legal amnesty and a path to citizenship for undocumented workers.

The law extended amnesty to any unauthorized immigrants who had lived in the U.S. continuously for the four previous years, who were willing to pay a one hundred eighty-five-dollar fee, and who demonstrated "good moral character," meaning they had no criminal record. They could apply for permanent legal status, and then, after eighteen months, become eligible for permanent resident, or "green cards," if they learned to speak English. At the same time, Congress moved yet again to beef up border security using surveillance technology. The law called for a 50 percent increase in border agents, although it didn't allocate the funds to hire them.

The legislation also attempted to enact stricter restrictions and sanctions on employers who hired illegal immigrants. It made it unlawful for companies to knowingly employ undocumented immigrants or to hire workers without properly checking their identity and eligibility.[10] The business lobby convinced lawmakers to water down those provisions, defanging the law's employer accountability provisions. To avoid sanctions, employers only had to ensure that an employee's I-9 form, created by the 1986 immigration reform act to verify immigration status, "reasonably appears on its face to be genuine."[11] However, employers also could be penalized if they scrutinized the forms too closely or questioned too aggressively a worker's naturalization status. As a result, most employers did little more than make sure they had an I-9 on file for every worker. In the first few years after the law took effect, the biggest immigrant-employing industries—construction, agriculture, and landscaping—faced public speculation that they ignored the paperwork rules. Many began using subcontractors. Because "subs" weren't employees, employers didn't have to worry about obtaining an I-9, and under the IRS rules passed in 1978, they also didn't have to pay them benefits or overtime.

The 1986 reform created legal status for 2.3 million immigrants who were in the country illegally at the time.[12] Many who previously feared deportation opted to stay in the United States and apply for visas. While the law was supposed to stop the further influx of Mexican immigrants, it didn't. In 1986, the Border Patrol's rate of illegal immigrant apprehensions was twenty-two per thousand. After the law passed, the rate fell to eleven per thousand in 1988, but as the legalization program wound down, as specified by the law, illegal immigration began to rise again. Worsening economic conditions in Mexico coupled with improving opportunities in the United States drove a new influx of Mexican workers. By 1996, the apprehension rate had reached seventeen per thousand.[13]

Just as Texas had been shielded from much of the economic stagnation of the 1970s, its oil-based economy caused the effects of the 1980s bust to linger far longer than in the rest of the country. Construction workers laid off by Marek saw little relief from their industry's slump. Instead, many found jobs in other fields or in other parts of the country as the national economy recovered elsewhere. Most of those who left the business wouldn't return even after construction rebounded in the 1990s. Combined with the fading union ranks, the flight of these mostly Anglo workers created an opportunity for a new, largely immigrant and non-union workforce. It also laid the foundation for a growing shadow economy that would engulf the construction industry and ensure that illegal immigration would remain a divisive political issue for the next thirty years.

6

Rise of the Independents

As America entered the 1990s, the recession began to dissipate. Interest rates stabilized, a technology boom began to unfold, and the economy enjoyed steady expansion and low unemployment. Texas once again was growing faster than any other region of the country, but the Anglo workers who'd left the construction business during the previous decade didn't return. Even though they were no longer bound to collective bargaining agreements, most commercial construction companies kept the same wage and benefit structure they'd had under the unions.

On the residential side, more subcontractors began classifying workers as "independent contractors," under the IRS rules adopted in 1978. Although the IRS has a strict twenty-point test for determining if a worker is an employee or an independent contractor, enforcement was scant. "It is by far the most abused change in the history of the IRS," Stan said. Increasingly, Marek found itself competing against subcontractors who had no employees. They "subbed" their work to their former employees, who were now all operating as independent contractors. The shift meant that the subcontracting firms paid no payroll taxes or benefits. Those burdens now fell on the workers. Overtime became a thing of the past. "Employers loved it because they could just send a Form 1099 to the worker and not have the record-keeping and responsibility of an employee," Stan said.

In 1991, the Texas Legislature made a final change that would essentially end full-time employment for residential construction workers. At the behest of major homebuilders, lawmakers overhauled the state workers' compensation insurance program, which lowered average premiums for employers. The move also increased competition in the insurance market and reduced legal battles over workplace injuries. The changes benefitted employers, but they were detrimental for employees. The number of years for which injured workers could receive wage replacement was capped at two, fees increased, and so did the denial of claims. Additional restrictions essentially shut down any recourse in the courts for workers who wanted to challenge these changes.

Many construction companies simply stopped covering on-the-job injuries. After all, most workers were independent contractors, and under that arrangement, their injuries were their problem. Each had signed a waiver saying they would provide their own insurance for work-related accidents. Few did. As a result, when workers were hurt on the job, they went to the nearest emergency room. Because of their inability to pay, they were classified as "indigent." Hospitals are required by law to provide certain percentages of indigent care. Injured, uninsured construction workers helped fill the quotas, which were subsidized by local taxpayers. "Taxpayers are the ones picking up the bill while the developers of the projects enjoy the cost savings," Stan said.

Within a few years, the residential construction industry had significantly streamlined its cost structure at the expense of the health, safety, and financial well-being of its own workforce. By switching to "independent" subs and eliminating overtime pay and accident insurance, Stan estimated employers could slash their costs by about 25 percent a year. "It was just too big of a competitive advantage to overcome," he said. "It just took off, and either you joined in the practice or you went out of business."

On the residential side of the business, Marek fought the changes, but eventually the company begrudgingly moved away from an all-employee workforce and adopted a mix of subcontractors and hourly employees to remain competitive. However, Stan insisted that subcontractors follow the same standards Marek applies to its own employees. He still bristles at the situation, which he believes weakened protections for residential workers, and it has made him all the more determined to ensure similar changes don't come to the commercial side of the business.

The legal workers who'd left the business in the 1980s found the industry's new labor structure less attractive. They were used to overtime and benefits and a chance to advance. With no career path, many found jobs in other industries rather than return to their old line of work. Older workers retired. Concerned that the industry would face a severe labor shortage, Marek spearheaded an effort in the mid-1990s to recruit new workers to construction. Known as the Construction Workforce Coalition, the group sent representatives to schools, job fairs, prisons, boot camps, and other potential sources of employees. It participated in welfare-to-work programs and even joined with the military in efforts to integrate veterans into the workforce. A decade after it began, CWC shut down. "We could not identify any measurable success in getting people into our industry," Stan said. "Instead, during this time that CWC was expending so much effort to attract American citizens, it was the immigrant worker who lined up to fill out applications."

For Stan, the CWC experience underscored a growing reality: The future of the construction industry depended on immigrant labor. "One of the misconceptions out there is that immigrant workers are taking jobs from American citizens," he said. "That is simply not the case, and we have our own experience to tell us that."[1]

As demand for labor picked up in construction and other industries in the 1990s, the number of immigrants crossing the southern U.S. border illegally again began to rise. After the 1986 reforms, the rate of illegal immigrant apprehensions fell by 48 percent during the next three years, to about 890,000. Then, apprehensions began rising again, reaching a peak of almost 1.7 million in 2000, according to the U.S. Border Patrol.[2]

The growing number of immigrants as indicated by apprehensions coincided with the decline in native-born construction workers between 1990 and 2001. One of every two new labor force participants during that time was an immigrant.

Technically, hiring these workers—regardless of their immigration status—didn't comply with the IRS's strict guidelines for independent contractors. For example, the IRS stipulates that contractors must set their own work hours, but in the construction business, workers had specific times they were told to report to a job. Nevertheless, enforcement of the contractor rules was scant and fell through the bureaucratic cracks of the federal government. Overtime violations, for example, are the purview of the Department of Labor's Wage and Hour Division, but the agency rarely audits an employer unless a worker complains. Construction workers, especially undocumented ones, rarely complained. Many had little reason to. They received their pay in cash, which meant their income was largely untraceable for tax purposes. As a result, they didn't have to pay taxes, and they didn't have any money withheld for health care or retirement benefits. It was all cash in hand.

The IRS, meanwhile, was responsible for tracking employers' payroll taxes. Proving a company was failing to pay its taxes required catching the firm misclassifying employees as independent contractors, then documenting in court that it failed to meet the standards of the twenty-point test. Even if the agency prevailed, the fines levied against the employer rarely justified the cost of the litigation.

By the end of the 1990s, the residential construction industry had become a virtual free-for-all in which the builders and construction companies had little connection to the workers they hired. While the employment conditions could be difficult, many Latino immigrants were happy for the work and were willing to forgo benefits and career paths to get a job. The arrangement boosted the profit margins for the industry while keeping the average housing costs in Texas 25 percent below the national average.[3] It also attracted illegal immigrants, because they could earn a steady income while operating under the radar of federal laws designed to prevent abuse of employment practices. As a result, homebuilding in Texas and many other states became a haven for workers who lived in a shadow economy, one that thrived on cash payments, scant paperwork, and few questions.

– – – –

Stan was at a breakfast meeting for the Houston chapter of a building trades group, the Associated General Contractors, the morning of September 11, 2001. He noticed people suddenly looking at their pagers and Blackberries, then dashing from the room. As the speaker ended his remarks, someone stood up and declared that America was under attack. A stunned silence settled over the group. No one knew exactly what that meant, but they quickly moved to find the nearest television. Someone turned on the news and the image of the twin towers of the World Trade Center engulfed in flames and smoke filled the screen. Stan knew instantly that the course of American history had taken a frightening and dramatic turn. What he didn't realize was that the crumbling towers of the World Trade Center would bury immigration reform for more than fifteen years.

George W. Bush had made reform a legislative priority, and he had the backing of a broad base of Republicans and Democrats. Bush, the former Texas governor who spoke fluent Spanish and whose sister-in-law was Latina, had both the conservative credentials and first-hand experience to guide the change. In his first trip outside the country as president, Bush flew to Monterrey to meet with Mexican President Vicente Fox. On September 4, 2001, Fox and Bush gathered at a summit in Washington to hammer out key points of an immigration reform package. "They're rolling out a ten-cannon salute and they're talking about immigration reform," attorney Charles Foster, who worked with Bush on the reform effort, recalled. "I'm thinking this is a done deal. Bush has all this goodwill with the Republican party; the Democrats were in favor. It was just working out the details. It was a very heady time."

In the wake of the terror attacks a week later, progress toward reform abruptly ended. The Bush administration created the Department of Homeland Security, which in addition to responding to future terrorist threats also took over the Immigration and Naturalization Service and the Border Patrol. As the government stepped up anti-terrorism efforts, politicians conflated security measures with immigration law. Fears of another attack on American soil grew. "After 9/11, the restrictionists were able to hang their hat on national security," Foster said. "Before, [their stance] was 'let's secure the border because these people are taking our jobs.' And now it was 'these people are coming to kill us.' Their mantra became 'we can do nothing until we secure the border.' Well, that's like saying we can do nothing on domestic policy until we eliminate all crime."

Before 9/11, employers simply had to attest to employees' immigration status. Now, they could be prosecuted for hiring undocumented workers. The new Homeland Security Department stepped up raids on private workplaces to search for illegal immigrants. The number of raids jumped to thirty-six hundred in 2006 from just five hundred in 2002. Immigration advocates protested because ICE, the Homeland Security division that enforced immigration law, often instituted raids without building a case against employers. In other words, while workers may have been deported, employers had no incentive to change their hiring practices.

A decade before the 9/11 attacks, the North American Free Trade Agreement had envisioned economic prosperity among the U.S., Mexico, and Canada through the free movement of people and goods across national borders. After the attacks, the Bush administration made immigration enforcement a synonym for fighting terrorism. The Homeland Security Department received a flood of federal funding, much of which it spent on deporting illegal immigrants. And one of the most fertile places to round up illegal immigrants was job sites. "They'd surround a job, and people would run like quail," Stan said. "They'd catch some, and they'd take them off to a detention center."

By 2011, the number of deportations had almost doubled, to four hundred thousand people. Yet the influx of illegal immigrants swelled as migrants fled economic hardship and violence not just in Mexico but in Central America as well. Between 2000 and 2008, the number of undocumented residents in the U.S. rose from an estimated 8.5 million to 12 million.[4]

Workplaces chafed under the increased enforcement. Employers were supposed to verify employment or risk prosecution or fines, but at the same time, federal anti-discrimination laws prevented them from refusing to hire someone they suspected of being undocumented if the worker presented papers that appeared authentic. The 1986 reforms required employers to complete a Form I-9 for every new employee they hired and verify the residency of workers. Each worker had to provide a Social Security card and another form of identification. The law stipulated that the documentation must appear to be legitimate, but it stopped short of requiring employers to verify the authenticity. After all, most human resources departments don't have a forgery expert on staff. With the advent of the World Wide Web, the government introduced E-Verify, an Internet-based system that compared workers' I-9 forms against other government records. Participation in the system remains scant—in most industries, adoption rates are below 12 percent of all employers.[5] E-Verify does little to root out undocumented workers because of its reliance on Social Security cards, which are easily forged. Fakes are readily available to anybody who wants to buy one.

During the 2000s, thousands of undocumented workers purchased their imitation Social Security cards at the nearest flea market for twenty dollars. In fact, between 2006 and 2010, dozens of people chose the same identity: Todd Davis. Davis, who is white, founded LifeLock, a company that claimed to protect consumers from identity theft. LifeLock's marketing blitz included ads in hundreds of newspapers and websites, as well as billboards nationwide displaying Davis' own Social Security number in large numerals. The campaign was supposed to show that LifeLock's product was so safe, Davis could publish his personal information without fearing identity theft. (In fact, he had his identity stolen at least thirteen times, and the company ran afoul of the Federal Trade Commission and thirty-five state attorneys general for false advertising claims.)[6] What Davis and the company didn't expect was that forgers would use his Social Security number to create fake cards for undocumented workers trying to dodge E-Verify scrutiny. "When he put out his social, it made it really easy for people to figure out his date of birth, and once you had his date of birth, you just get an ID made with your picture and his date of birth and his social on it—you'll clear E-Verify," said Jacob Monty, the Houston immigration and labor attorney who represents companies with large Latino workforces. At one point, Monty had found one hundred sixty-five different illegal immigrants using Davis' identity, often pasting their own picture on an ID with Davis' name and birthdate.

Illegal immigrants who didn't become Todd Davis had no trouble adopting other identities. Some used the Social Security numbers of their native-born children. Others tapped prisoners who were willing to sell their Social Security numbers to raise money for their families while they were incarcerated. Puerto Rico was fertile ground for fake cards. "That was counterfeit paradise," Monty said. "You had a whole island of U.S. citizens that had Spanish surnames, and they could sell those names to Mexicans in the U.S. who needed fake documents—and they cleared E-Verify."

If the Department of Homeland Security found that a worker had provided a fake Social Security number or other ID, the employer was notified and given ninety days for the employee to fix the problem. If the situation couldn't be fixed—in most cases because the worker was undocumented—the employer had to fire the worker, who was rarely, if ever, deported.

"I firmly believe that most employers don't know that the people are undocumented," Monty said. "Undocumented people look like the rest of us. They speak perfect English, often times. Many of them were brought here as babies." Most employers aren't equipped to ferret out false documents beyond obvious forgeries. Monty had two former ICE agents working for his law firm, and some of the fake IDs were good enough to fool them, he said.

Even more troubling for employers like Marek, the law doesn't require any follow up by the government. In other words, if Stan found undocumented workers on his payroll, he had to fire them, but that didn't mean Homeland Security would deport them. In fact, the law often drove workers further into the shadows. They were ineligible to work legally, yet they were still in the country. One former Marek employee, who asked to be identified only as "Hector," had worked for the company for thirteen years when a review by Marek's health insurer found his identification didn't match his Social Security number. He was making about sixty-five thousand dollars a year as a finishing foreman, supervising crews of as many as thirty-five people doing drywall on large commercial projects around Houston. He was working at the job site when he got a call to return to the office. His supervisor told him about the documentation mismatch. Hector had three months to resolve the problem. "I said, 'it's not something I'm going to be able to fix,'" Hector recalls. Like so many others, he had bought his Social Security card at a flea market.

Over the years, Hector has had thousands of dollars in Social Security taxes withheld from his paycheck for a benefit he will never receive. The Social Security Administration collects billions of dollars a year in taxes from unknown people—those whose W2 forms from their employers don't match any Social Security numbers. The agency has about three hundred forty million of these unclaimed W2s, dating back to 1937. But in the past decade, the number has surged by more than 25 percent, a jump that researchers attribute to undocumented workers.[7] Illegal immigrants contributed one hundred billion dollars to the Social Security system from 2004 to 2014, according to Stephen Goss, the administration's chief actuary. Yet many receive few if any benefits from their contributions.[8]

U.S. citizens are hurt by a system that fails to identify and tax all workers. As aging Baby Boomers retire, putting a strain on entitlement programs, Social Security and Medicare have become increasingly dependent on this unclaimed revenue from illegal immigrants.[9] "You could say legitimately that had we not received the contributions that we have had in the past from undocumented immigrants ... that would of course diminish our ability to be paying benefits for as long as we now can," Goss told MSNBC in 2014.

A two-wage earner couple retiring in 2010 who paid Social Security and Medicare taxes their entire working lives would have contributed $722,000 in payroll taxes but would have received $966,000 in benefits, according to a 2012 study by the Urban Institute. In other words, citizens and legal residents will cost the system, on average, $244,000 per household,[10] while Hector and other undocumented workers are contributing $12 billion and withdrawing nothing.

Hector finds himself in a convoluted, yet not uncommon, situation. His parents brought him to the U.S. from Matamoros, Mexico, in 1984, when he was five years old. His parents obtained legal status under the 1986 reforms, but they incorrectly completed his paperwork. He has lived in the country ever since, working for Marek Brothers, buying a home, and raising four children. Various attempts to untangle his legal status have failed.

Facing the three-month deadline to fix his Social Security issue, Hector worked "until the last minute" at Marek and then took a two-week vacation. He got a job doing finishing work for a labor broker earning twelve dollars an hour—half what he made at Marek. He missed the higher pay, but he also missed the family work environment of his old employer. After a few years, he decided to start his own business renting party equipment. He now employs seven people, all with legal status, even though he himself remains undocumented. He has a tax ID number for his business and makes sure he pays payroll taxes for his workers. "I pay taxes," he said. "I follow the rules. I have car insurance. I do everything I'm supposed to do. I even have a fishing license," he said, pulling the folded document from his wallet.

Hector's predicament has played out thousands of times in similar ways across the construction industry. The increased scrutiny after 9/11 only drew more attention to the growing number of undocumented workers. In response, many employers simply moved more workers off the payroll. To Stan's dismay, some commercial subcontractors did wind up following the lead of their residential counterparts and began classifying more employees as independent contractors. This shift cleared the way for even more egregious practices, such as the construction industry's expanding reliance on labor brokers to help find workers. The shadow economy began to swell.

– – – –

After Hurricane Katrina tore through the Gulf of Mexico in 2005, construction companies intensified their reliance on labor brokers to provide crews to rebuild the battered Gulf Coast. These brokers functioned as middlemen between workers and employers and often charged exorbitant fees to bring workers to the U.S., both legally and illegally. The immigrants' temporary work status—and the large portion of their pay they surrendered to the brokers—often meant they couldn't repay their debts. Even brokers who hired workers already in the country typically didn't offer benefits or withhold taxes. In fact, most paid in cash. Ironically, the post-9/11 crackdown that required employers to thoroughly vet their new hires was contributing to the rise of brokers who used off-the-books and often undocumented immigrants. This was just one of the immigration issues that Barack Obama would wrestle with during his two terms as president.

When Obama took office in 2009, it was clear that immigration reform would be an uphill battle. The Great Recession from 2007 to 2009 left millions unemployed. Many Americans blamed illegal immigrants for taking American jobs and adding to the country's hardship. To get a Republican-dominated Congress to consider overhauling immigration policies, Obama increased detentions, deportations, and employer raids to show his political opponents he wouldn't simply grant amnesty to undocumented workers as the Reagan administration had. Nonetheless, Congress did not pass a comprehensive immigration bill during Obama's tenure.

The Great Recession hit the construction industry almost as brutally as the downturn in the 1980s had. By 2009, office vacancy rates in the biggest Texas cities were as high as 23 percent, and investment in commercial real estate fell 80 percent from the previous year. By the time the recovery began to take hold, labor brokers had become a fixture in the commercial construction business, especially in the interior trades such as drywall. A 2013 study by the Workers Defense Project and the University of Texas found that of the two thousand construction workers interviewed in the state, more than half were undocumented, 60 percent had no workers' compensation insurance, and 40 percent were classified as independent contractors rather than employees.[11]

This was not the outcome Stan's father and uncles had envisioned when they started Marek Brothers almost eighty years earlier. The company resisted using labor brokers. It still preferred to hire and train its own teams. Stan concluded that labor brokers and off-the-books workers were jeopardizing the future of the construction business, and he was determined to do something to save it.

7

A Pathway to Failure

Stan made an optimistic gesture in 2013 to underscore his belief that immigration reform was essential for companies and the labor force: He ordered a custom license plate for his Ford Expedition — CIR13. The shorthand reflected his commitment to "comprehensive immigration reform." The license plate was inspired by an effort in Congress, led by lawmakers from both parties, to overhaul immigration laws. Known as the "Gang of Eight," they proposed sweeping changes on everything from border security to a pathway to legal status for eleven million illegal immigrants.[1] Given the broad support, many lawmakers, and Stan himself, were confident about reform. "I thought that bill was going to pass," he said.

A year after Stan got his license plate, it became clear that not only would Congress fail to enact reform, the issue of immigration had become as politically polarizing as abortion and gun control. The bill failed, largely because of politics, but the outcome also reflected a growing backlash toward immigrants and any effort that made it easier for them to gain legal status. Beginning in 2005, Stan had become increasingly active in political circles around the issue of immigration reform. He focused on granting immigrants some type of legal status that would bring undocumented workers out of the shadows while requiring their employers to withhold taxes. A lifelong Republican, Stan started by donating to congressional candidates from both parties who supported his views. He quickly decided that simply donating to politicians wasn't enough to make his ideas heard. While Stan had become outspoken on the need for legal status and taxation, he felt that rational calls for reform were drowned out by opponents who simply wanted to deport all illegal immigrants. Business and industry were too quiet on an issue that profoundly affected their own economic well-being. Just as he had spearheaded the Construction Workforce Coalition, Stan enlisted some of his fellow construction industry executives and formed Texans for Sensible Immigration Policy, or TxSIP, in 2006.

"Our position is simple," Stan wrote to his employees at the time. "Immigrant workers who have migrated here are meeting a huge portion of our demand for workers. Since there has been virtually no legal method for them to come here and work, many have come illegally and then secured false documentation in order to get hired." For Stan, the argument was simple economics: Illegal immigrants were meeting a need in the workplace that others, despite a decade of recruitment, simply wouldn't. Therefore, it made sense to provide them legal protection to continue working, while ensuring the country was collecting the full tax revenue from their income.

CWC's failed efforts already showed that the industry couldn't fill its jobs with American citizens. Most native-born children wanted to go to college and, increasingly, settle into white-collar jobs. Schools no longer encouraged students to pursue craft work, which was seen as physically demanding, unreliable, and unsafe.

"Our industry still needs additional workers to meet its needs even with the immigrant workforce that's here," Stan wrote. "So, we want the ability to keep the working relationship we have without having them shipped back." Losing those workers would "devastate our companies, our industry, and our economy."

The federally mandated limit on visas may have contributed to the influx of illegal immigrants, but many of those workers had been here for decades now. Some, like Hector, had been brought to the United States as children and raised here. They were embedded in the economy and the benefit of their labor was taken for granted. Douglas Holtz-Eakin, president of the conservative American Action Forum and former director of the Congressional Budget Office, estimates that illegal immigrants account for about 6 percent of the country's gross domestic product. Yet much of the rhetoric about illegal immigration ignored this economic reality.

TxSIP wanted to improve the visa system so that it better reflected demand and allowed for immigrants to come to the U.S. legally to contribute to future growth. The group called for a foolproof identification system, rather than the easily spoofed pairing of Social Security cards and photo IDs. It pushed for better border security and a thorough vetting of people entering the country. TxSIP also stressed that it wasn't advocating amnesty or a path to citizenship for illegal immigrants nor did it want illegal immigration to continue unchecked.

TxSIP focused on the economic relationship between immigrant workers and higher-paid citizens. Without construction workers on the job site, for example, hundreds of architects, engineers, estimators, project managers, purchasing agents, and others would lose projects and perhaps even their jobs. TxSIP continued to take its message to members of Congress, but it also began lobbying the general public.

By 2012, TxSIP had gained enough influence that it succeeded in helping to beat back more than a hundred laws that would have stepped up deportations and separated immigrant parents from their native-born children, said Norman Adams, Marek's long-time insurance agent and an outspoken reform advocate who serves as the group's executive director. Before that, Adams had met with Democrat Nancy Pelosi, then, as in 2020, the speaker of the U.S. House of Representatives, and convinced her to use the term "sensible immigration reform." But the immigration issue only became less sensible and more polarized. "It's become popular to think that any support for immigration makes you a Democrat," said Adams, who, like Stan, is a lifelong Republican. "Republicans are ignoring the economic issues of immigration."

Stan also helped form Americans for Immigration Reform. This group of business leaders favored many of the same reform initiatives as TxSIP, but the new team focused on employment issues such as improving the E-Verify system and streamlining hiring practices for employees with legal status. Stan further provided seed funding for TexasGOPVote, a website for a discussion of the party's ideals that, not coincidentally, focused on immigration reform. He traveled to Washington frequently to meet with members of the Texas delegation and others who he hoped would support the reform efforts.

When the Gang of Eight—among them Democratic senators Charles Schumer of New York and Richard Durbin of Illinois and Republican senators John McCain and Jeff Flake of Arizona, Lindsay Graham of South Carolina, and Marco Rubio of Florida—introduced their legislation in 2013, many lawmakers reacted favorably. House Speaker John Boehner, a Republican who'd succeeded Pelosi two years earlier, praised the move, expressing confidence that Republicans and Democrats "can find common ground to take care of this issue once and for all." The effort had something unusual going for it: It had no significant opposition. Business leaders, law enforcement, and most organized religious organizations supported the plan.

Congress had tried and failed to pass broad immigration reform for years but in a different political climate. In 2007, President George W. Bush dusted off his pre-9/11 proposal. Bush made it clear that any change had to involve some path to citizenship or legal status for undocumented residents. "There are some who would allege that the best way to deal with eleven to twelve million people is to get them to leave the country," Bush said. "That's impossible."

At that time, Democrats showed little interest in supporting Bush's initiative, in part because organized labor, one of the party's key constituencies, still saw immigrants as a threat to union jobs. Meanwhile, the pattern of job-site raids had continued, which alienated many Republican businessmen who might have supported the effort.

The raids disrupted businesses and scared workers, many of whom fled and never returned. One of the highest profile raids came in December 2006. About a thousand ICE agents descended on six Swift & Company meatpacking plants in Utah, Colorado, Nebraska, Iowa, Minnesota, and Texas as part of a ten-month investigation known as "Operation Wagon Train." As the agents filed into the plants and ordered the assembly lines stopped, workers, at least in some cases, were divided into two lines based on the shade of their skin. Those with darker complexions were detained and questioned. Almost thirteen hundred workers were arrested for immigration violations and identity theft related to falsified IDs, and many were later deported.

The raids left a lasting impact on the communities where the plants operated. As word spread, Latinos near the Swift site in Greeley, Colorado, seemed to vanish, either abandoning their homes or hiding in their basements. Classrooms suddenly were half empty after rumors spread that ICE was coming for immigrant children next.[2]

The Swift crackdowns were the largest workplace immigration raids in history. More followed in other parts of the country, including Houston. Less than two years later, in the pre-dawn hours of an April morning on the north side of town, a convoy of about fifty federal and county vehicles surrounded the manufacturing plant for Shipley Do-Nuts, which operates stores in Texas and five other southern states. A helicopter hovered overhead as ICE agents swarmed the factory, bringing workers out in handcuffs and arresting twenty suspected of being in the country illegally. Shipley, a family company like Marek, had been in business for seventy-two years. One worker at the scene, who wasn't arrested in the raid, commented: "For those immigrants who don't have documents, these raids bring fear."[3]

Employers were worried, too, but the government was counting on that fear. In a meeting with administration officials, Stan claims an adviser on Bush's staff told him that the raids would continue until more businesspeople backed changing immigration laws. "He said, 'we're going to make it miserable for you' until you support reform," Stan maintains.

The administration's view was clearly focused on using employers as a means to ferret out undocumented workers. After the Swift raids, Homeland Security Secretary Michael Chertoff said: "When businesses are built upon systematic violation of the law or others go to systematically violate the law in order to either bring in illegal migrants or to allow them to find jobs, that is a problem that we have to attack."[4]

Bush had hoped that stepped-up enforcement would be a start toward reviving the immigration reform effort he'd envisioned when he came into office the January before the 9/11 attacks. But seven years later, he was deep into his second term. After the invasion of Iraq and the failed response to Hurricane Katrina, Bush lacked the political capital in Congress to push a reform bill through. The measure succumbed to grass-roots opposition, much of it fueled by talk-radio extremists like Rush Limbaugh. Many members of what would become the Tea Party faction in the Republican Party bristled at the idea of reform, especially if it cleared a way for illegal immigrants to become citizens. They remembered Reagan's effort in the 1980s that gave amnesty to millions of illegal immigrants yet did nothing to seal the border. The ranks of the undocumented had more than doubled since then, and the anti-immigrant sentiment had risen sharply among the Republican base.

President Obama ended the workplace raids and replaced them with audits. "It was the stupidest thing they could possibly do," Stan said. While audits were less divisive for immigrant families, they exacerbated the problems in the construction industry because workers who had been on payrolls, contributing Social Security taxes and buying homes, were forced underground. "Now they're working for cash and not paying payroll taxes," Stan said.

The audits were supposed to target employers who knowingly hired illegal immigrants, and ICE issued fines as a deterrent. But many employers complained that they were subjected to fines even if they had no undocumented workers on their payroll because ICE auditors would cite them for clerical errors or other paperwork flaws. ICE has refused to release details of its audits. It has not said how many undocumented workers it has found or what happened to them after they were identified.[5]

The political winds seemed to be shifting by 2013, even as business frustration with audits simmered. Republicans had lost the 2012 presidential election—Mitt Romney received only about 25 percent of the Hispanic vote—and GOP leaders vowed to rebuild the party by making it more inclusive. Unions, too, had changed their tune. As union ranks continued to decline, labor leaders began seeing immigrants as potential members who could help them beef up their numbers.

With both Boehner and Obama supporting change, crafting and passing a law appeared to be a straightforward political exercise. Bipartisan groups allied for innovations. They had been working on the framework of immigration reform almost since the failure of Bush's plan in 2007. The efforts intensified after the 2012 election, but the strategy was basically the same: Tighten border security and loosen restrictions on legal entry to reduce future illegal immigration and meet workforce demands. Then identify a method by which undocumented workers already in the country could achieve legal status—the so-called "path to citizenship."

While the pathway provision remained controversial, both sides agreed on a compromise: Undocumented residents would face an eight-year period before they could gain permanent residency. In the meantime, they could apply for legal status that would allow them to live and work in the U.S. without fear of deportation, provided they didn't break the law.

The Obama administration welcomed the opportunity for a bipartisan bill. But the president had angered some Democrats by stepping up deportations to win favor with Republicans who had accused him of being soft on illegal immigration. As lawmakers began negotiations, the reform effort became ensnared in a more hotly debated piece of legislation—"Obamacare," the president's signature health care overhaul officially known as the Affordable Care Act. Representatives from both parties agreed that immigrants seeking legal status should pay for their own health care. But Obamacare eliminated the cheap, catastrophic coverage that gave immigrants a low-cost option. Republicans didn't want taxpayers funding any portion of immigrant health care, and Democrats argued that without some sort of public subsidy, millions of migrants would be forced to file bankruptcy or leave the country.

Reform moved forward in the Senate. Stan concentrated much of his political arm-twisting (he didn't like hiring lobbyists or relying on trade organizations) on Texas's junior senator at the time, Republican John Cornyn. Stan printed business cards with the heading "Sensible Immigration Reform." The cards had no contact information for Stan, but on the back, they read "call Senator Cornyn" and gave the politician's Washington office number.

Stan met with Cornyn several times, hoping the lawmaker would help galvanize the Senate's support for the measure and, in turn, put pressure on the House to follow through. Cornyn offered an amendment calling for tightening border security, but it failed. In June 2013, the Senate passed a sweeping reform bill by 68–32. Fourteen Republicans crossed the aisle to vote with Democrats, but Cornyn voted against it.[6] Many senators, though, supported the bill only because they sensed that the appetite for reform in the House was slowing.

Congressional Democrats knew that if lawmakers couldn't reach a deal, the administration was prepared to address immigration reform through an executive order—Obama's tool of choice when he couldn't get cooperation from Congress.

Meanwhile, the House dragged its feet. Boehner refused to consider reform unless he could bring a bill to the floor under the "Hastert rule." Named for former House Speaker Dennis Hastert, a Republican from Illinois, the rule required that new legislation must have the support of a majority of the party that presented it before it came up for a vote. Facing mounting opposition from core Republicans opposed to immigration reform, Boehner didn't have the party majority required under the rule to put reform to a floor vote.

Stan's custom license plate became obsolete—2013 came and went without comprehensive reform. In fact, opposition to reform picked up. Stan and many other Republicans didn't realize at the time that a little-known political outsider named Steve Bannon, and Breitbart, the right-wing news website he supported, had decided to attack the Republican establishment. Immigration was their weapon of choice. Bannon and Breitbart tapped into a deep-seated opposition to immigration reform among working-class Republican voters.

Bannon chose House Majority Leader Eric Cantor's re-election campaign as the vanguard for his assault on the old Republican guard. Cantor was one of the most powerful members in Congress and a supporter of immigration reform. His challenger was an unknown college professor, Dave Brat, who was polling thirty points behind Cantor heading into the Republican primary in Virginia. Bannon stoked up right-wing talk radio, working hard to portray Cantor as favoring "amnesty" for illegal immigrants. Within a matter of weeks, Brat went from a distant challenger to a significant threat. In June 2014, he upset Cantor by a staggering eleven points. Immigration opponents touted the election results as a referendum on the national reform effort, and Republican leaders got the message. "Dave Brat proved this issue moves votes," said Ken Cuccinelli, the former Virginia attorney general who's the Trump administration's acting deputy secretary of homeland security. "In terms of Republicans... it was a turning point on the immigration issue." (With Cantor's defeat, Bannon moved on to finding a candidate to back for the 2016 Republican presidential nomination, and he found one in Donald Trump.)[7]

Two weeks after Brat's victory, a wave of unaccompanied minors from Central America turned up on the U.S.–Mexico border, making headlines and strengthening the resistance to reform. Obama pushed ahead with an executive order to keep undocumented parents of American-born children from being deported. The state of Texas challenged the order, a federal judge upheld the challenge, and the U.S. Supreme Court—with one vacancy on the bench—split 4–4, letting the lower court's decision stand.[8]

Stan, who'd had multiple meetings with Boehner, still bristles at the outcome. "That was a good bill, but it got nowhere," he said. "If Boehner had taken it to the House for a vote, it would have passed by 60 percent. If we'd had an immigration bill in '13, we would not have this problem [now] and the Republicans probably wouldn't have run Donald Trump."

Jacob Monty, the Houston immigration attorney and a Republican who initially supported Trump (he no longer does), said his party bears the blame for failing to enact reform. "It's a Republican problem to be sure," he said. "That's where the bottleneck is." It's particularly frustrating, he said, since Republicans led the way on the last major immigration reform effort in 1986.

Not all Republicans agree. Dan Crenshaw, a GOP congressman from Houston, said his party has been willing to consider compromise on immigration issues; it's the Democrats who have been intransigent. "The Democrat Party has moved radically away from us," he said. "I don't think we've moved, but I think they have.⁹"

Despite Stan's multiple trips to Washington and his high hopes for progress in immigration reform, he ultimately returned to Houston dejected. He'd been sure that the politicians would do the right thing. Instead, those he had supported and those he had worked with in his own party had succumbed to political gamesmanship and, as he saw it, fear. The Tea Party, which was largely an ideological movement advocating American supremacy, fiscal conservatism, and limited government, now controlled the Republican agenda. It opposed any legal status for undocumented workers and its hard line left little room for pragmatism. Stan got rid of his SUV, with its CIR13 plates, and bought a new vehicle. Its license plate bears a random, state-issued combination of numbers and letters.

He wasn't ready to give up, but he knew the fight had gotten a lot more difficult, and he needed to change tactics.

Section II

Fixing Immigration

8

A Broken System

Immigration became a hot button issue in the 2016 presidential election. Yet, despite its pervasiveness and the polarity it exacerbated, the subject sparked little serious discussion. Those who opposed reform developed several pat responses. Many asserted that the problem wasn't legal immigration, only *illegal* immigration. Foes often expressed sentiments such as "I have no problem with immigrants, as long as they come here the right way." The implication is that today's immigrants are doing something differently from those who entered through Ellis Island starting in the late 1800s. Many Americans want to believe there's a line to enter the country, and anyone who wants to come should simply wait his turn. While it may be a comforting notion, it's not how the system works.

"Sometimes you hear people saying 'well, get in line like everybody else.' What they don't realize is that there is no line," said Tony Payan, director of the Mexico Center at Rice University's

James A. Baker III Institute for Public Policy. "The poor people, they have no path to come to this country."

Another common retort to immigration is even more simplistic: "What part of illegal don't you understand?" Unfortunately, few Americans really understand the laws surrounding immigration. Most native-born citizens have had little direct contact with the immigration system. What's more, immigration law is so complex it has been compared to tax policies and even to King Minos's mythical labyrinth in ancient Crete that housed the Minotaur.[1]

To understand why the immigration system is broken it helps to first learn how it currently works. The 1965 reforms created four types of immigration: Family reunification, employment, refugees and asylum seekers, and the diversity lottery program.

Almost two-thirds of immigrants to the U.S. gain access through family reunification requests. This route requires a permanent U.S. resident or legal citizen to petition for the newcomer. They can appeal only for spouses, parents, children, or siblings. First Lady Melania Trump used this method to gain U.S. citizenship for her parents in 2018 even as her husband, President Donald Trump, has derisively referred to the method as "chain migration."

Spouses and children get priority in family reunification. Each country of origin receives a number of visas that is capped, similar to the old quota system. There's a waiting period that can range from a few years to more than twenty-five. Mexico, for instance, has a wait time of seventeen to twenty years.

Employment also can provide legal entry into the country. Immigrants with a college degree and in-demand skills can receive legal entry if they identify an employer who's willing to offer them a job. Employers must petition the government for the visas, but only after they prove they have advertised the job and couldn't find any American citizens to do it. The petition process can take as long as two years. Only if the work visa is approved can the would-be immigrant apply for permanent residency, or what's commonly called a green card. The best-known examples of work visas are called H-1Bs and are widely used for workers with advanced skills in fields such as technology and medicine.

Congress limits the number of these visas. Currently, sixty-five thousand are issued each year. As of March 2020, though, about two hundred seventy-five thousand people applied, meaning employers sought to hire more than four times as many workers than there were visas.[2] "Lots and lots of things stand in the way between somebody who wants to come here to work, or an employer who needs a worker, and a legal pathway to do it," said Ben Johnson, executive director of the American Immigration Lawyers Association.

Getting the visa doesn't ensure a green card. That requires a separate application that mandates a medical exam with a blood test, a mental health review, an inquiry into whether the applicant has ever abused drugs or alcohol, and even an assessment of the person's tattoos. It also includes an examination of their family and work histories. The background check can take three years or more.

Refugees and asylum seekers must demonstrate that they have been persecuted or have reason to fear persecution in their home country because of their race, religion, nationality, political opinion, or membership in a particular social group. The number of these refugees accepted legally has declined. In 1990, the U.S. admitted 120,000; by 2016, that number had fallen to 85,000. President Obama proposed raising the ceiling to 110,000 in 2017, but the Trump administration reversed course, slashing the number to 30,000 by 2019.[3] Trump has said he plans to lower the number even further.[4]

The final path to entry is the diversity visa lottery program. It issues fifty thousand visas a year to immigrants who aren't required to have a family member or a sponsor such as an employer in the United States. More than one million people annually apply. Applicants must have a high school diploma and two years' work experience. The program is open only to immigrants from countries that have sent fewer than fifty thousand people to the United States in the past five years. That rules out Mexico, Canada, China, Brazil, and other high-profile nations. President Trump has called for eliminating this route after a man from Uzbekistan who came to the U.S. under the program in 2010 was accused of running down pedestrians and cyclists on a New York City bike path in late 2017.[5]

"To enter the country legally is [a] limited opportunity," said Ali Noorani, executive director of the National Immigration Forum in Washington. "To go through the multiple steps necessary, to pay the fees to get to legal permanent residence, is incredibly difficult."

While the 1965 and 1986 reforms originally were designed to create avenues for legal entry, in reality, the laws have failed to keep pace with the country's changing economic and political realities. "Because of these long backlogs and waits, even if there's a line you theoretically can get into, how many people are going to wait twenty or thirty years for a visa?" asks Theresa Cardinal Brown, director of immigration and cross-border policy for the Bipartisan Policy Center, a Washington-based think tank. "If you're in really desperate straits, that's really not a viable means for you to try to come in."

The work visa programs are available for highly skilled workers. For lower-level laborers, temporary work programs or visas don't exist. Despite manpower shortages in construction and agriculture, the immigration system essentially denies any legal access to workers in such fields. Would-be immigrants without family relationships or the skills that may convince an employer to sponsor them have no way to enter the country legally, even when they're needed to fill waiting jobs.

Immigrants historically have been vital to boosting the U.S. workforce. And in turn, this expanding labor pool has bolstered the nation's economy. Immigrants and their children have accounted for more than half of American workforce growth during the past twenty years. That number is likely to rise during the next two decades, according to Robert Kaplan, president of the Federal Reserve Bank of Dallas.[6] While the 2020 coronavirus outbreak has temporarily upended the employment picture, most economists expect these long-term trends to continue.

As the country's unemployment rate fell below 4 percent in 2018, Stan Marek and other construction industry managers grew increasingly desperate for workers. Eighty percent of contractors nationwide reported having problems filling positions such as carpenters, painters, and drywall hangers, a study by the Associated General Contractors of America showed. Few employers expected the situation to improve in the coming year, and most said they were forced to raise prices and stretch out time schedules. Put simply, the labor shortage caused homes and offices to cost more and to take longer to be built. The culprit? Industries are caught between a lack of available domestic labor and restrictive policies that prevent hiring foreign-born workers legally.[7]

"It doesn't make sense, but I guess the law is not meant to make sense," said Jill Campbell, an attorney with Baker Ripley, a Houston nonprofit that assists immigrants in Houston. "The law is meant to just restrict who comes to the United States."

Even with record unemployment after the economic lockdowns in response to the coronavirus in early 2020, few expected native-born workers to take jobs picking strawberries, working in slaughterhouses, or hanging drywall. In fact, the government designated many of these workers as essential to the economy without considering whether they were in the country legally.

– – – –

In 2015, Stan gave a speech to a group of students at his alma mater, Texas A&M. The students were about to graduate with degrees in construction science. Stan spoke to them about the state of the workforce they were going to encounter and the impact of the broken immigration system. The realities of the job site could only be experienced first-hand, and despite four years of study, Stan felt the students were unprepared for what they would face. As the talk ended and the small gathering dispersed, he noticed a young Latina waiting on the side of the room. As the last of the well-wishers left, she approached him cautiously, checking again to make sure everyone had departed before she asked his advice.

She had just completed a year-long internship with a construction company in Houston and would soon begin her own career in the industry. She struck Stan as a hard-working, ethical young woman, and she was in a quandary. She had recently encountered a troubling situation on the job site where she had interned, and she wanted his advice.

The woman had worked for an electrical contractor on a big construction project. The general contractor was one of the largest in town and had an excellent reputation for quality and safety. But one of the major subcontractors on the job had supplemented its hourly workforce by hiring a staffing company. Staffing companies are common in many industries to help fill short-term employment gaps. Construction is the same. But after four decades in that business, Stan knew there was a difference between a true temp agency, which followed proper hiring and worker classification rules, and a labor broker, which generally paid people in cash for piecework and classified them as independent contractors to avoid payroll taxes. As a result, labor brokers were magnets for undocumented workers. The brokers asked few questions in the hiring process, but they also offered workers few recourses. It seemed to Stan that the problems the woman was witnessing fit the description of how labor brokers often operate. She told Stan that the staffing company was shortchanging workers in their pay and forcing them to work in unsafe conditions. The workers approached her because she spoke Spanish and they had nowhere to turn. They wanted her to relay their concerns to her managers, who spoke only English.

The story the workers told her was disheartening. Of the sixty-member crew hired by the general contractor to complete the building interiors, about forty-five worked for the labor broker masquerading as a temp agency. They were undocumented and earned fourteen dollars an hour. The fifteen documented workers hired by the same contractor were paid twenty-two dollars an hour for the same work. Also, the undocumented workers were told to put in overtime because the job was behind schedule. However, they were not offered the time-and-a-half compensation the legal workers got. Nor were they provided workers' compensation insurance. The broker told the crews if they tried to get workers' comp, they would be deported, the woman told Stan. They lived under the constant threat of deportation—a fear that the labor broker exploited.

The young woman wanted to help the workers but didn't believe she could approach the general contractor or the electrical contractor she worked for. After all, she could jeopardize her own job opportunities if she rocked the boat. She was disturbed by the workers' plight yet felt helpless to do anything about it. Unfortunately, Stan told her, there wasn't much she could change on her own.

"I've been doing this for forty-seven years," he said. "I've seen this industry deteriorate from all union to open shops to this. This is as bad as it's ever been. These workers at lower-tier subs are trapped."

The situation deteriorated after the recession of 2008 as more illegal immigrants began moving from residential to commercial construction seeking better pay. At the same time, commercial operations themselves sought the cheaper workers that labor brokers could provide to reduce costs. Commercial drywall is far more complicated than residential. Homebuilders use wood studs, and the process for hanging sheets of drywall is largely the same throughout every job. Residential drywall subcontractors typically use local crews, many with undocumented workers, and pay them based on the number of feet of wallboard they hang each day. The workers simply screw the wallboard into the studs until all the sheets are gone. Commercial buildings, by contrast, can have as many as fourteen kind of studs, eight types of drywall, furr downs, drop ceilings, and other characteristics that require special attention. The residential drywall model, with labor brokers paying by the foot rather than by the hour, doesn't work in the more complex commercial world. It would mean paying the drywall hangers exorbitant sums for hourly work, boosting overall building costs.

Big construction companies have found that the labor broker system also can create plausible deniability if a worker's legal status becomes an issue. If a lower-tier contractor uses undocumented workers, the general contractor can claim it had no knowledge of the hiring practices of the sub.[8]

Of course, not all labor brokers skirt immigration laws by offering undocumented workers for hire. Some simply adhere to the letter of the law, if not the intent. Most brokers set up a business with their own tax identification number. Then they hire the workers needed for a job. These workers—both legal and undocumented—are typically considered independent contractors themselves. As such, they don't have to be carried on the subcontractor's workers' compensation policy and are not covered if they're injured on the job. Most general contractors mandate that their subs have workers' comp insurance, but this covers only employees. It does nothing to help contract workers. The broker also is required to obtain a certificate proving he has an insurance policy, even if he never pays claims on it because he, too, is supplying contract workers for hire. The arrangement meets the language of employment law, even if the contract workers are not covered.

Technically, the contract workers are responsible for their own insurance, but few buy it. For Stan, this is a prime example of what's wrong with the system.

The Houston market shows how this system shortchanges workers. A labor broker can provide a worker to a contractor for twenty-two dollars an hour. In some cases, the broker may be paying the worker as little as twelve dollars an hour, giving the broker a huge profit. On some jobs, brokers may have a hundred people working for them. They don't pay overtime, and in fact, most of the workers don't realize they should be receiving it. Those who know about overtime rarely ask for it because they don't want to draw attention to their immigration status. A comprehensive 2020 study found that as many as 21 percent of construction workers nationwide are either misclassified as contract workers or paid off the books, and many of them are undocumented.[9] Even if workers file a complaint, the Department of Labor, which investigates overtime fraud and other illegal labor practices, seldom shuts a broker down. At the first hint of an investigation, brokers typically either sell their business to someone else or shutter it and start over with a new tax ID number.[10]

Brokers convince the workers they hire to sign a contract saying they're working independently and recognize they are responsible for paying their own taxes. They also sign a waiver for workers' compensation insurance under the 1991 Texas state law that altered insurance requirements for the industry.

Sometimes, brokers hire other brokers, creating another layer between the general contractor and the undocumented workers on the front lines. The deeper the layers go, the more difficult the trail becomes for regulators to follow. The rules governing independent contractors are complex, and even if construction companies wanted to change them, the firms are likely to find few allies. Too many other companies rely on independent contractors of one type or another and don't want to see the laws reversed. California, for example, passed a law in 2019 that said workers could only be considered contractors if they perform duties outside the usual course of a company's business. The law was designed to give so-called gig economy workers the same benefits—such as overtime pay and health insurance—as employees. In May 2020, the state sued the ride-sharing companies Uber and Lyft and accused them of violating the law by classifying workers as independent contractors, which the companies deny.[11]

When an economy increasingly relies on independent contractors it creates a problem for states as well as businesses. In Texas, because neither brokers nor the workers they hire are paying payroll taxes, the state's unemployment insurance fund suffers. If the fund faces a deficit, as it did in 2009 when it came up almost seven hundred fifty million dollars short, the state must increase the tax on businesses to make up the shortfall.[12]

Heading into 2020, the condition was even more dire. Texas's unemployment fund was well below the minimum adequate solvency level recommended by the Advisory Council on Unemployment Insurance, meaning the state would be unlikely to get through a recession without additional federal support. Indeed, as jobless claims surged — they would top three million, far higher than the two hundred thirteen thousand claims for the same period in 2019 — Governor Greg Abbott requested additional interest-free federal loans to pay claims.[13,14]

"Because we don't have a guest worker program, the economy created one, and it's a black market," said Houston immigration attorney Jacob Monty. And it's supported by a massive enterprise that is making money off the undocumented for everything from fake identification to smuggling the workers into the country.

Overburdened government agencies lack the resources to address the problem. The companies that benefit from the system have little incentive to change it. Even workers who risk being taken advantage of are willing to live with it. They sign on with labor brokers because they can avoid paying taxes by not reporting income to the IRS. They don't receive overtime pay, but they typically can work longer hours to boost their take-home earnings. "Latinos are entrepreneurs," Stan said. "They want to work as much as they can. But when they come here and they're just starting out, the only resource they have is their own body. As they get older, they realize 'hey, my body's wearing out.' Then what do they do?"

While the system holds short-term financial benefits for the workers, brokers, and companies involved, Stan maintains it costs the construction business over the long term. Industry studies show that during the past twenty-five years, productivity has fallen 50 percent. Stan and others attribute the plunge to a lack of training. Brokers don't verify the skills of their workers, and many undocumented laborers essentially learn on the job. "They're paying the same wage, and the productivity is half what it was," Stan said. "If you're working by the sheet, you're going to throw it up as fast as you can, whether it's good or it's bad." If the Sheetrock work is bad, someone must fix it, which costs money.

Untrained workers have contributed to a 400 percent increase in labor costs during the past four decades, but the workers who do the jobs haven't benefited. The hourly rate for a Texas carpenter has plateaued at about fifteen dollars during the same time. That's largely because work has to be redone to fix mistakes, said Chuck Gremillion, executive director of the Construction Career Collaborative, or C3, an industry group that Stan helped form to improve working standards. "The way the industry solved the problem was just throwing unskilled labor at it," Gremillion said.

Labor brokers don't emphasize job safety the way true contractors do. "Safety has a price," Stan said. "When you have a safety culture, it costs something. Now, it pays for itself if you're providing workman's comp. It lowers your insurance costs because you have fewer accidents. But all these people in the shadows have no safety training. They're having more accidents, and that impacts them, and it impacts their families. The problem is too many building owners really don't care. They want a low price."

Stan believes this culture is unsustainable. The construction industry is mortgaging its future for short-term gains, flying in the face of the lessons Stan learned from his father, and propping up a shadow economy. "It's definitely a race to the bottom in wages, in training, in skills," Stan said. "If you have employees, you invest in them. You treat them differently." That investment includes providing better skills training and safety education. Labor brokers, on the other hand, see workers as commodities, he said. "They take a hands-off approach because the workers aren't employees," Stan said. "So, they don't get safety training, and if they don't do good work, the brokers just fire them and get somebody else."

An influx of immigrants by itself doesn't lower wages. Pay in the unlicensed sectors of the building trades—excluding plumbers, electricians and others licensed by the state—has fallen largely because of the labor broker system and the lack of immigration reform, Stan said. In many cases, undocumented construction workers sign on with labor brokers for substandard wages because it's the only choice they have. Lower wages ripple through the job market, pulling down salaries for higher-skilled work, and ultimately spreading over the entire economy. If the starting rate for a carpenter drops to twelve dollars an hour from twenty, the decrease also cuts the rate for more experienced workers, or for those in more skilled lines of work. The result: Everyone is making less than they would in a market without shadows.[15] A 2013 study by the University of Texas and the Workers Defense Project found that 52 percent of all construction workers are unable to meet their families' basic needs.[16]

"When the wages are higher, productivity gets higher because all of a sudden, you're paying by the hour, you've got employees you're investing in, you do a little more training," Stan said. "You're building a labor force."

The Texas construction market is uniquely hurt by another reality—competition from the petrochemical industry. The arc of the Gulf Coast from Beaumont, an hour east of Houston, to Corpus Christi, about four hours to the south, has the highest concentration of petrochemical plants in the world. In recent years, as hydraulic fracturing significantly lowered the price of natural gas in the United States, more chemical companies have been expanding facilities in the greater Houston area, siphoning off some of the most skilled construction workers. That leaves the building industry scrambling to fill jobs. "They get the cream of the crop because their wages are so much higher," Stan said of chemical companies and their employees.

Undocumented workers often fill the lost construction jobs. For them, low wages may be better than no wages, even if employers are blatantly ripping them off. One in five construction workers has been denied pay for work they've done, often referred to as "wage theft," or "payroll theft." Most who fall victim to this practice are afraid to speak up for fear of being deported. There's a broader economic impact, as well. In Texas, the state loses an estimated $54.5 million annually in tax revenue from payroll fraud.[17] As the labor broker system drives down wages and prices fall, more drywall contractors are turning to brokers to stay competitive. "The labor brokers are proliferating," Stan said. "You shut one down and three more open up. There's no stopping them."

Marek and other companies that try to stick to their principles find themselves tempted by the shadow system to stay competitive. "It is a real mess, and all because of the lack of an immigration bill," Stan said.

Without immigration reform, Marek and others are left to navigate the unintended consequences of immigration and tax policies that hurt employers and workers alike. "You've got honest employers trying to do the right thing with every incentive to cheat and do the wrong thing," said Norman Adams, the TxSIP director. "It's damned if you do and damned if you don't if you try to follow the law on immigration."

— — — —

Stan takes pride in the immigrant success stories among the diverse workers in his own company. It's common to find thirty- or forty-year veterans among the hundreds of immigrants in its ranks. As he got to know his team, he grew more certain that the national debate about immigration didn't reflect the complexity of the issue.

One Marek executive, Jorge Rodriguez, came to the United States from Mexico illegally with his parents in 1978. When he was five years old, his mother and father loaded the family in an old station wagon, threw a blanket over Jorge and his siblings in the back seat, and headed north. Jorge remembers the car rumbling along a dirt road as the family crossed into Arizona, where Jorge's father found work on a ranch. A year later, the family moved to Texas.

In 1985, his father befriended a retired lawyer who offered to help the Rodriguez family get green cards. With the 1986 immigration reforms, his family was granted legal status. Jorge grew up in Texas, finished high school, graduated from Texas A&M, and married. He joined Marek in 1997, rising to the top ranks of the company. He knows he was lucky to enter the United States at a time when laws provided his family a way to work and live in the country legally. Without immigration reform in 1986, Jorge might have wound up like Hector, the Mexican immigrant who Stan was forced to let go in 2009. "The only difference between Hector and me is a piece of paper," Rodriguez said.

Another senior Marek executive, Saied Alavi, said immigration policies have failed to keep up with the realities of illegal immigration. Immigrants like Hector present one of the most difficult problems, because they had little say in their immigration status, and have never known their home country. "People were brought here, and they're American. They don't know any better," said Alavi, Marek's director of operations. "They went to school, they got educated—and they're still illegal." Alavi has little patience for people who say Latinos should wait to immigrate until they get a visa. Given current immigration laws, that could take decades. Many are fleeing government oppression, gang threats, and drug violence. They don't have the leisure of waiting for the bureaucratic wheels of the antiquated U.S. immigration system to grind along. "If you are in a desperate situation, you're not going to wait," Alavi said. "That's why they come across."

The Department of Homeland Security grants about ten thousand visas a year for low-skilled workers from Latin America.[18] If all eleven million illegal immigrants were deported and forced to wait for visas to return to America, it would take more than a thousand years just for those already here to come back to the country again legally. And that assumes none has children or a spouse, which most do.

"When people say all they have to do is go back and get in line, you would measure that line in centuries," said Charles Foster, the immigration attorney.

Alavi had first-hand experience with the broken immigration system. He came to Houston as a refugee from Iran after the fall of Shah Mohammad Reza Pahlavi in 1979. Although he had two engineering degrees and had served as an officer in the Iranian Navy, as a refugee he was desperate for any work he could find. He wound up taking a spot as a security guard at a Marek warehouse, working from midnight to 8:00 a.m. and looking for engineering jobs during the day. After a few months, when one of his bosses discovered his engineering background, they offered him a chance to help with some bookkeeping. Eventually he approached the general manager about doing something else. "He asked, 'what do you know about Sheetrock?'" Alavi recalled. "I said, 'I have no idea what that is.'" He agreed to work for a few months hanging drywall, while still handling his bookkeeping duties. Once he got familiar with the product, he returned to the company offices and worked his way up. "They gave me opportunity, and as I did more, they put more in front of me," Alavi said.

Today, Alavi tries to reflect those same values in overseeing Marek's workforce. The company's history only underscores Stan's irritation with the broken immigration system. He knows that current laws prevent capable workers who have needed skills but lack proper documentation from contributing to the broader economy.

"In times of low unemployment, having qualified undocumented workers that you can't hire because of their status, only adds to the frustration," Stan said. "Those workers and their employers are going to find a way to meet the demand of a booming economy, at the detriment of companies that try to follow the law."

9

Beyond Construction

No metropolitan area showcases the country's changing demographics better than Houston. America's fourth-largest city is at the vanguard of the shift from a white majority to a "minority-majority" society. From 1960 to 2010, its population almost quadrupled, to 4.1 million from 1.2 million. Anglos were responsible for little of the growth. In 1960, 74 percent of the city's residents were white; five decades later, that percentage had slipped to 33 percent. Meanwhile, the Latino population ballooned from 6 percent to 41 percent.

"No city has benefitted more from immigration than Houston," said Stephen Klineberg, founding director of the Kinder Institute for Urban Research at Rice University. "How different the story of Houston would have been, had we not been a magnet for new immigrant growth."

Houston's immigrant population has put the city squarely in the middle of the reform debate. Economists have long known that immigration fuels economic growth. For every 1 percent increase in the immigrant population, GDP rises by 1.15 percent, according to a 2017 estimate by Moody's Analytics for ProPublica.[1] Immigrants also fill labor shortages in specific industries, as Mexican workers did for American agriculture during World War II and as they are doing in construction now. Increased labor helps lower prices for consumers. And while undocumented immigrants place certain financial burdens, primarily on state and local governments, their economic benefits tend to exceed their costs over the long-term.[2]

Economies benefit when more people are available to work. When population growth stalls, productivity suffers. Since the Great Recession of 2008, productivity growth in the United States—the increase in the amount of goods produced by the same number of workers—has been stagnant, averaging just 1.1 percent annually. That compares with a 2.1 percent average from 1960 to 2000. Americans are having fewer children—in 2019, the U.S. birth rate dropped for the fifth-straight year to a thirty-five-year low—and the country's working-age population has stagnated during the past decade.[3] Adding new members to the workforce is crucial. "The surest way to increase the working-age population is through immigration," said Neel Kashkari, president of the Federal Reserve Bank of Minneapolis. "Immigration has boosted U.S. economic growth throughout history and can continue to do so if the country remains committed to openness and opportunity."[4]

Few cities may understand this better than Houston. Immigrants are drawn to the city for its employment opportunities. Between 2000 and 2012, the city added five hundred thirty thousand jobs, leading the nation in expanding employment, despite the Great Recession. This was true even as Texas provides less funding than other states for social safety nets such as for programs to support indigent children, the mentally ill, and the disabled.

Yet demand for low-skilled workers in Houston and across the United States still outstrips the labor supply. Dennis Nixon, CEO and chairman of International Bancshares Corporation, estimates that the U.S. needs to add between six hundred thousand and six hundred fifty thousand low-skilled workers a year to maintain 2 percent growth.[5] The high unemployment of the 2020 coronavirus pandemic did little to change this demand.

Undocumented job seekers are filling the gap in many industries. A statewide study found this group generates a net thirty-three billion dollars in government revenue and indirectly contributes to the creation of 3.3 million new positions in Texas. Yet despite these contributions, the country is once again beset by concerns that immigrants are taking American jobs. "You better be smart, and you better be tough, and they're taking your jobs and you better be careful," then-candidate Donald Trump told the Conservative Political Action Conference in 2014.[6]

The fear is almost as old as the country itself and there's never been any evidence to prove it. Most undocumented immigrants take jobs that require low skill levels, strenuous manual labor, or both, in such fields as construction, agriculture, housekeeping, and maintenance. "Those are jobs that have been done by immigrants throughout our history," attorney Charles Foster said. "Italian immigrants built the skyscrapers and subway tunnels of New York; Chinese immigrants and Irish immigrants built the railroads. We have an agriculture industry because of immigrants. Without that, we would be dependent on importing all of our foodstuffs, and that would be a national security issue."

If immigrants were "taking" these jobs from Americans, then every workplace that ICE agents raid would unleash a flood of U.S. citizens applying for jobs that the undocumented lost. That hasn't happened: No native-born Americans are lining up for work at meat processing plants, dairy farms, or for that matter Stan Marek's drywall warehouse. Even the high unemployment in the wake of the 2020 pandemic did not result in large numbers of native-born workers applying for these types of physically demanding jobs. In fact, many undocumented immigrants who work in agriculture, meatpacking, construction, and other industries were deemed essential during the pandemic. Tony Payan, at Rice University's Baker Institute for Public Policy, said the pandemic response underscores the paradox facing undocumented workers. "They're considered essential workers and yet they have no status," he said. In some cases, their wages were reduced even as they were expected to stay on the job, even after COVID-19 was detected in some meatpacking plants and other job sites. "A lot of that labor is these undocumented workers who have stayed working, who have risked their health and their life," he said. "And so they're already part of the very hard-working workforce in this country."[7]

There's little evidence that an influx of immigrants pushes Americans into unemployment. "What we do find is that by having more immigrants in the U.S., it increases the supply side of the economy, which means there's more people working and making things—but it also increases the demand side, which means there's more people buying things. [That] also increases the demand for production and products made by workers, which increases salaries and jobs," said Alex Nowrasteh, senior immigration policy analyst for the Cato Institute, a free-market-oriented public policy research organization. "That [increased demand] mostly goes to employ Americans, so if you take out that consumer, you're destroying job opportunities elsewhere."[8]

Most economic studies find that undocumented immigrants do not drive down overall wages for native-born Americans. The one review that did, by Harvard economist George J. Borjas in the 1990s, showed a slight effect on native-born workers from immigrants entering the workforce, but only for those who were high-school dropouts. Their wages fell by about 1.7 percent over twenty years while most other native-born workers' wages rose by about 1 percent. Far from replacing Americans, immigrants— both documented and undocumented—are supporting them. Just as Klineberg's studies revealed that the white population's growth in Houston has remained little changed for decades, the same is happening across the country. "Immigrants add population, and therefore they add economic activity, and therefore they add economic growth," said Rice University's Tony Payan.

The U.S. population is aging rapidly, and without immigrants to replenish the workforce, economic growth will slow. That's already happening in Japan, the world's third-largest economy. More than 20 percent of the country's population is over age sixty-five, and by 2030 that number will increase to one in three, economists predict. Combined with a declining fertility rate, some of Japan's biggest companies, such as automakers and electronics manufacturers, may find it difficult to attract manpower. The International Monetary Fund estimates that the aging population could drag down the country's gross domestic product by 1 percentage point in the next three decades. "A rapidly aging population and shrinking labor force are hampering growth," the IMF said. Given that outlook, Japanese policy makers adopted an immigration reform package in 2018 designed to attract three hundred forty-five thousand foreign workers by 2023.[9,10]

U.S. citizens depend on a rising population to fund the entitlement programs they rely on. "We have a lot of dependencies on our workforce," said Theresa Cardinal Brown at the Bipartisan Policy Center in Washington. "Our Social Security system and Medicare system are pay-as-you-go, not you get what you paid. So everybody who's working now is paying for everyone who's getting benefits now. If there aren't enough people working when I retire then I'm not likely to get any benefits."

Immigrants, even at the lowest levels of the economy, boost growth when they are recognized and allowed to participate fully. Latinos in the United States legally participate in the labor force in greater percentages than whites: 67.2 percent compared with 62.2 percent. Yet, the undocumented who are anxious to join the workforce face an array of restrictions that keep them in the shadows and create hidden costs to society. For one thing, they can't get a driver's license—the key to mobility and financial stability. In 2015, almost 22 percent of the 39.7 million Americans living in poverty were Latino.[11] About 16 percent didn't have basic financial services like a checking account,[12] and many were "credit invisible," which means that the three major credit reporting agencies have no records on them. Many Latino households either rely on no credit or the generosity of friends or relatives. Without established credit, many can't access traditional sources of capital such as mortgages and car loans. Such limitations mean they contribute less to the formal economy.

– – – –

In 2005, Stan Marek began formalizing his suspicions about the upheaval in his industry by studying illegal immigrants and how they had disrupted construction. What he identified reinforced his own experience: A complex web of social, economic, and political issues had emerged, and the way the country was reacting to it didn't make sense. He found that border states such as Texas pay the most taxpayer-funded benefits for illegal immigrants. But by blocking a pathway to legal status for these immigrants, states increase the chances that their U.S.-born children will depend on welfare programs. Rather than providing relief for taxpayers, the process further raises the burden. (While undocumented workers aren't eligible for welfare, their U.S.-born children are.)

Stan concluded that illegal immigration has its broadest impact in three areas: education, health care, and law enforcement.

Ninety-one percent of native-born Americans have at least a high school diploma, compared with just 62 percent for non-citizens. As a result, Hispanic and Latino immigrants accounted for 42 percent of the country's unskilled labor force in construction, agriculture, hospitality, janitorial services, and similar low-skill fields. The old axiom that immigrants "do the jobs we won't do" is largely true. Unskilled immigrants tend to focus on certain types of physical labor. Highly educated immigrants are equally selective, favoring jobs as scientists, medical professionals, or computer designers over careers as lawyers, judges, or educational administrators.[13]

The short-term costs of keeping immigrants in the shadows are easier to see than the long-term consequences. In 2009, 57 percent of households with children under eighteen that were headed by at least one immigrant parent (legal or illegal) used at least one welfare program, compared with 39 percent for native households. If immigrant children were barred from taxpayer-funded education, that dependence was more likely to extend to a second generation, increasing the poverty rate and expanding the underclass. Failing to educate immigrant children would create an expensive cycle of welfare dependence.[14]

A landmark 1982 Supreme Court case, Plyler v. Doe, required that states provide public education to all children through grade twelve regardless of their immigration status. By 2011, educating illegal immigrant children cost taxpayers nationwide an estimated fifty-two billion dollars annually, with most of those expenses borne by state and local governments. Justice William Brennan, who wrote the majority opinion in the Plyler case, argued that the cost of educating the undocumented is far lower than the cost of maintaining an uneducated lower class of society.

But those costs are not insignificant. From 1995 to 2012, the percentage of public-school students with at least one undocumented parent rose to 6.9 percent from 3.2 percent.[15] And the burden isn't limited to border states. Almost 12 percent of the public-school students in New York City are undocumented minors.[16]

Illegal immigration impacts higher education, too. Eighteen states have provisions to extend discounted in-state tuition to undocumented students. Two states, Alabama and South Carolina, prohibit illegal immigrants from enrolling in any college or university. Arizona, meanwhile, does not offer cheaper in-state tuition for undocumented students. By contrast, in Texas, a hotly debated law championed by former Republican Gov. Rick Perry provides financial aid to undocumented students.

As Stan sees it, U.S. educational policy has compounded the rise of immigrant labor in the building trades. President George W. Bush in 2002 signed the No Child Left Behind Act, which measures school performance based on how well students are prepared for college rather than for a vocation. Between 1990 and 2009, the vocational credits earned by public high school graduates declined by 15 percent, to 3.6 from 4.2, while average credits for core academic fields for college preparation—English, math, science, and social studies—rose, according to the National Center for Educational Statistics.[17] Fewer students entered the trades, leading to an overall decline in available labor for industries such as construction.

At the same time, wages in construction have shown only modest gains, even with a worker shortage. In Texas, the average construction worker earned $18.27 an hour in 2016,[18] according to the U.S. Bureau of Labor Statistics, compared with $16.43 in 2011.[19] The combination of stagnating wages, a decrease in training, and disinterest from U.S. workers left many construction jobs to be filled by undocumented workers. They were willing to accept lower pay, and often were less prepared for the jobs.

Undocumented immigrants who take jobs that lack medical insurance have strained the U.S. healthcare system. Arizona estimates it pays more than five hundred million dollars a year to provide medical access for the illegal immigrants who account for 37 percent of its uninsured. Nationally, the cost of emergency room treatments to Medicaid topped two billion dollars annually in 2013, mostly for undocumented immigrants, according to Kaiser

Health News.[20] About two-thirds of illegal immigrant adults were uninsured as of 2017.[21] Many use emergency rooms as their primary care provider, contributing to a 36 percent national increase in ER visits from 1996 through 2006. Hospitals have struggled with rising costs from uninsured patients, which has stretched staffs, raised billing expenses, curtailed services, and even closed some maternity wards and trauma centers.[22]

Not all studies paint a dire picture of the drain undocumented immigrants pose. These findings suggest that because illegal immigrants pay more than $11.6 billion annually in state and local taxes, such as sales and property taxes, these individuals more than offset the $5.5 billion in non-Medicare expenses they impose on the public health care system each year.[23,24]

Police organizations also must juggle both sides of the immigration debate. They have concerns about illegal immigration's effect on crimes from drug and human trafficking, to prostitution, gang violence, and identity theft. But law enforcement officials also argue that requiring them to enforce federal immigration laws that can lead to arrest or deportation has hampered their efforts to build trust within communities. Critics claim that "sanctuary cities" like Houston, in which city leaders don't cooperate with federal immigration raids, essentially offer amnesty to undocumented workers. But local police say that when they serve as de facto border patrol agents, their job of keeping communities safe becomes more difficult.

When Texas passed a bill banning sanctuary cities in 2017, police chiefs from some of the state's largest cities objected. The bill allowed police officers to question the immigration status of anyone they detain, including for routine traffic stops. "We knew it would create the perception that law enforcement had become ICE agents," Houston Police Chief Art Acevedo said. The number of sexual assaults reported by Hispanics in Houston fell by almost 43 percent after the law took effect, at least in part because the

victims feared local cops would arrest them for immigration violations. Acevedo's department engaged in extensive community
outreach to reassure Hispanic residents that the police weren't
there to deport them. "We had to let them know that people become cops to chase crooks, not day laborers," he said. "It was a bill
in search of a problem that didn't exist." Houston police already
worked with federal immigration officials to arrest and deport
those with a criminal record, he added.[25]

Some native-born Americans worry about illegal immigrants
committing crimes. This may be a red herring. Generally the undocumented break the law at a lower rate than the native-born
population. A study by a team of sociologists at four universities
found that immigrant populations increased in the one hundred
thirty-six largest U.S. urban areas between 1980 and 2016, yet
crime rates stayed the same or fell.[26]

While critics often point to illegal immigrants as drug traffickers, there's a clear distinction between those who cross the border
illegally to work in the U.S., and those who are bringing drugs into
the country. "Most drugs—85 to 90 percent of them—come at
ports of entry in vehicles, trucks and cars, on bodies—*in* bodies —
they're coming right under the noses of [Border Patrol] agents,"
Payan said.

President Trump has talked up immigrant crime statistics.
He has especially pointed to the Salvadorian American street
gang, MS-13, making the moniker shorthand for immigrant crime
among his supporters. The Justice Department estimates there
are about six thousand MS-13 members in the United States, many
of whom came into the country as minors and either were already
gang members or joined after they arrived.[27] Trump speaks frequently about the gang, often linking it with sanctuary cities. Researchers have found no link between the two.[28]

Both the Obama and Trump administrations have focused
immigration policy on increasing deportations but rounding up

immigrants and deporting them isn't cheap. Deporting the estimated eleven million illegal immigrants already in the country would cost between two hundred billion and three hundred billion dollars, said Douglas Holtz-Eakin, president of the American Action Forum, a conservative think tank, and former director of the Congressional Budget Office. That's more than twice what the U.S. spends on homeland security annually.[29] Deportation would require about thirty thousand additional administrative judges and three hundred thousand beds in new detention centers, Holtz-Eakin estimates. "It's a lot of money; it's a lot of big government," he said. Assuming all the undocumented could actually be found and deported, the move would reduce the labor force by about 6 percent, likely triggering a recession, he predicted in 2017.[30] In 2007, Arizona got a taste of this economic impact when it cracked down on illegal immigration and its economy shrank by 2 percent.[31]

Perhaps the starkest example of the economic consequences of pursuing illegal immigration has been in Alabama. Between 2000 and 2010, the state's undocumented population soared from twenty-five thousand to one hundred twenty thousand as workers took jobs in agriculture, meat packing, and construction. State lawmakers grew frustrated with the federal government's inability to address the surge. They faced mounting public sentiment that, as one representative put it, "the illegals in this country are ripping us off." In 2011, the Alabama Legislature passed House Bill 56, considered the harshest immigration law in the country. The bill's sponsor boasted that it "attacks every aspect of an illegal alien's life." It banned landlords from renting homes to undocumented immigrants, required schools to check students' legal status, and ordered police to arrest suspected immigration violators. Motorists who picked up an undocumented hitchhiker could face criminal charges. The law even allowed private citizens to sue police officers for failing to enforce the mandates. Not surprisingly, illegal immigrants fled the state, as lawmakers intended.

Six weeks after the law was passed, police stopped a driver for an improper license tag on a rental car. The driver didn't have a license, only a German identification card. The law required police to arrest him, take him to court, and detain him until federal immigration authorities took over. The driver was an executive for Mercedes-Benz, which operates an auto manufacturing plant in the state. Soon after, a similar incident occurred with another auto industry executive, this one from Honda. The business community began to fear that the law not only would drive immigrants from the state but push out major employers as well.[32]

The law took effect during Alabama's fall harvest. Many farmers who relied on Mexican labor for field work saw their crews flee almost overnight. Brian Cash, whose family farmed tomatoes on one hundred twenty-five acres on Chandler Mountain in northern Alabama, watched his field crew decline from sixty-four to eleven in one day, then vanish completely over the next few weeks. He tried hiring American citizens to replace the workers he'd lost—only two people applied, and he caught them inflating the amount of produce they picked to drive up their wages. Tomatoes rotted on the vines. A few weeks later, Cash plowed them under. He estimated his losses for the season at one hundred thousand dollars. "It's going to be a little while, but eventually people will see what has been done here," he told The Guardian newspaper. "The cost of food in the supermarkets is going to go up, and in the end we will all pay the price." [33]

Even before the farming disruptions, the law began causing unexpected problems in the state. Churches worried that their Spanish-language masses or soup kitchens for the poor could run afoul of the law if they unknowingly accepted illegal immigrants. Utilities wondered if they should cut off service for customers they suspected of being undocumented. Some county attorneys questioned whether citizenship papers were required for using public swimming pools—a bitter reminder of the state's segregated history.

The law put a financial burden on small police departments, which had to devote more time and money to immigration enforcement. In some cases, the additional workload meant paying officers overtime. In others, communities had to pay for jailing suspected immigration violators. Increasingly, members of the Latino community stopped talking to police. Crime victims went silent, fearing they would be victimized a second time by police who would arrest them for being in the country illegally.

By 2013, facing widespread outcry about the law's unintended consequences and an array of legal challenges, Alabama paid three hundred fifty thousand dollars to settle litigation and essentially rolled back many of the most onerous provisions.[34]

The lesson didn't last. Three years later many outside the state had forgotten the upheaval the Alabama law had caused. As the presidential campaign heated up, candidate Donald Trump set the tone by offhandedly referring to Mexican immigrants as drug traffickers and rapists. He vowed to round up all the undocumented workers, send them home, then seal the border with a wall that he would force the Mexican government to pay for. (Mexico never agreed to a wall, and Trump later asked Congress to appropriate eighteen billion dollars for it.) Other Republican candidates—except for Jeb Bush—began jockeying for the staunchest anti-immigrant stance. It was no longer politically feasible to advocate for the sort of reasonable reform efforts that Stan Marek and other business leaders had championed just three years earlier. Meanwhile, American business owners remained trapped in the middle—they struggled to find enough low-skilled workers, and many of the ones they did hire lacked legal status and faced possible deportation.

In the decades since the Mareks founded their company, U.S. immigration policy has done an about-face. During World War II, the U.S. government recruited Mexican field workers. Today, agriculture, like construction, is struggling with an incongruous immigration environment. The U.S. needs immigrants to keep production rising, yet it institutes hurdles to their presence. Economists at Texas A&M University found in a 2015 study that immigrants account for 51 percent of all dairy workers, and dairies that employ immigrants produce 79 percent of the U.S. milk supply. "Eliminating immigrant labor would reduce the U.S. dairy herd by 2.1 million cows, milk production by 48.4 billion pounds, and the number of farms by 7,011. Retail milk prices would increase by an estimated 90.4 percent," the study found.[35]

A labor shortage or price increase in one industry can ripple through the economy. When an employer in construction or agriculture can't find enough workers, job creation slows in other businesses. Conversely, a University of Virginia study found that every agricultural job created in the state led to 1.6 new jobs in other areas of the economy.

Anti-immigrant sentiment helped fuel Trump's rise in the Republican presidential primary, but immigration got little attention during his general election battle with Hillary Clinton. Stan Marek, convinced that Clinton would win and that the Democrats had little interest in serious immigration reform, prepared himself for four more years with little progress on the issue.

Donald Trump's victory shocked him. But he began to hope that as a real estate developer, Trump would adopt a more realistic view of immigration. "I can't imagine the president would be as anti-immigrant as he had to be to win the election," Stan said a few days after Trump's surprise win. "I think he knows who builds his buildings, cleans his rooms, and takes care of his golf courses." Perhaps with the election over, Trump would cool his campaign rhetoric, Stan thought, and advocate more rational solutions to fix the broken system of immigration. Once again, he would be disappointed.

10

The Wall

"When Mexico sends its people, they're not sending their best....They're sending people that have lots of problems, and they're bringing those problems with us. They're bringing drugs. They're bringing crime. They're rapists. And some, I assume, are good people."

Donald Trump, the billionaire New York real estate developer and former reality TV show host, offered those comments when he announced he would run for U.S. president. At the time—June 16, 2015—few took him seriously as a candidate. His inflammatory depictions of immigrants only underscored why so many political pundits thought he didn't stand a chance.

Trump wielded anti-immigrant rhetoric to play on fears harbored by many Americans. In some ways, he was tapping the same fervor that the Ku Klux Klan inflamed in support of the National Origins Act. Many on the far right of the Republican party dusted off the old, unsubstantiated arguments about immigrants—

they take jobs from Americans, they're a drain on welfare programs, they bring crime and unsavory elements into our society. But Trump's anti-immigrant orations also resonated with mainstream American factory workers, many of whom had lost jobs to their counterparts in foreign countries. Trump promised to put these Americans back to work. He vowed to build a two thousand-mile wall along the southern border. He told his followers that "Mexico is not our friend," and that "they're killing us at the border and they're killing us on jobs and trade." He stoked fears that "we don't know what we're getting" with illegal immigrants. At a campaign rally in Manchester, New Hampshire, he looked up at a plane flying overhead and remarked, "that could be a Mexican plane up there—they're getting ready to attack."[1]

Charles Foster, Stan Marek's immigration attorney, had advised both George W. Bush and Barack Obama on immigration policy. During the 2016 campaign, he worked first with Jeb Bush. When Trump won the Republican nomination, Foster teamed with Democrat Hillary Clinton to craft counterpoints to Trump's incendiary claims about immigrants. "I prepared all of her talking points on immigration for the debates, analyzing every nuance, every little thing Trump had ever written and said," Foster recalled. "I had prepared so many zingers and so many points showing that everything he said made no sense. There was never a substantive discussion. It was such a huge disappointment."

Trump promised large-scale deportations of illegal immigrants but never admitted that the government only had the money to deport at most 10 percent of the undocumented population.[2] Nor did he reveal how he would make Mexico pay for building a border wall, or, for that matter, who he would hire to build it. "If he's going to build a wall with legal workers in Texas, he's going to have a very hard time," Stan said. The industry already faced a labor shortage, and at least 20 percent of all construction workers nationwide were believed to be undocumented—in border states like Texas, the number was probably closer to half. The irony that Trump would have to rely on the very immigrants he was targeting to build his wall wasn't lost on immigration reform supporters.

Presidents as far back as Ronald Reagan have suggested a southern border wall. Portions of the border, of course, have been walled or fenced for years. But the notion of a physical barrier that people can see and touch can be reassuring, especially to those who believe that Latin American immigrants are bringing crime and drugs across the dividing line with them.

Stan knew that these beliefs were based in fear rather than in fact. About 40 percent of all illegal immigrants have simply over-stayed their visas. They didn't cross the border illegally. They came by plane, or bus, or boat, and they had a visa to do so. But when that visa expired, they just remained in the country.

"Rhetorically, the idea is that you can put up a wall to stop what people analogize to water—we talk about a flood of immigrants—so what do we build to stop a flood? We build a dam," said the Bipartisan Policy Center's Theresa Cardinal Brown. "The idea of a wall is a rhetorical device that is simple for a lot of people to understand. The truth is we are not being flooded with people."

You wouldn't know it from listening to the political rhetoric, but illegal immigration is near a fifty-year low. Illegal border crossings peaked between 1999 and 2000, when the Border Patrol recorded almost 1.7 million apprehensions. By 2017, that number had fallen to less than 311,000—a reduction of more than 80 per-cent. The level was the lowest since 1970, rising just slightly to 404,000 in 2018.[3] "Compared to where we were, we're in a very good place," said David Aguilar, former deputy commissioner for the U.S. Customs and Border Patrol.[4]

The government in both Democratic and Republican adminis-trations has expanded the ranks of the Border Patrol. Politicians have also increased spending on vehicles, equipment, and tech-nology such as drones, night-vision gear, and satellite imagery.

"What we have done has actually worked very well—boots on ground, sensors, agents, fencing where it's required," Rice University's Tony Payan said. "All these things paid off. We're not looking at a collapse of the border, we're looking at a turnaround of the border."

Funding border protection, however, has increased the cost for catching each illegal immigrant. "We haven't stopped to say, `wait a minute, how much is enough for every kilogram of cocaine and for every immigrant that we catch?'" Payan said. "For now, we're still throwing money at the problem."

If Border Patrol agents didn't have to spend their time detaining and processing "busboys and nannies" who are trying to enter the country illegally to find work, they could focus on apprehending the truly dangerous people who are trying to enter for nefarious purposes, said Tom Jawetz, vice president of immigration policy with the Center for American Progress, a left-leaning public policy institute.

Border support such as a wall should be measured, judicious, and tailored to the desired outcome—the prevention of illegal activity on a persistent basis in a given area, Aguilar said. "We should not be building infrastructure, be it walls, barriers, whatever, for posturing purposes."

The wall remains politically popular, a physical show of strength in our battle to secure our borders. As Payan points out, however, it's not clear what the wall would actually do other than generate political satisfaction for its supporters. Not only have the numbers of attempted illegal border crossings declined, but Border Patrol agents are apprehending 80 percent of those who try to cross. The bigger problem, Payan said, is that we have redefined immigration as a bad thing, and that blinds us to the economic need that only immigration can address.

"We've been manipulated politically for a very long time," he said. "It's a manufactured crisis that has given a lot of politicians political capital. In fact, we're about to create the opposite of an immigration crisis." The real crisis is the labor shortage that could result from poorly conceived immigration policy, he suggests.

– – – –

Trump's rhetoric may have been untethered to the realities of illegal immigration, but he spoke in the stark platitudes that anti-immigration voters wanted to hear. While George W. Bush had told the country that deporting eleven million undocumented residents would be impossible, Trump made it sound simple. "They will be out so fast your head will spin," he told television host Bill O'Reilly.

Trump's victory changed the tone of policy discussions and altered the sentiment in the immigrant community. Suddenly, immigrants felt even less safe. Department of Homeland Security memos released a month after Trump's inauguration outlined plans to use local law enforcement to augment immigration enforcement, called for fifteen thousand more border control and ICE agents, and defined anyone without proper papers as a potential criminal who could be deported. Those with pending deportation cases would be detained, rather than released.[5]

During Trump's first six months in office, deportations increased by 40 percent. ICE agents became more aggressive in arresting people. Local police officers in many communities detained immigrants pulled over on traffic stops or those found to not have driver's licenses. In public elementary schools, teachers reported an increase in bullying against Latino children—even those who were citizens. White classmates told these kids ICE would be coming for them or their parents. Fear swept over the immigrant community. "They're terrified," said Jill Campbell, an attorney for Baker Ripley, the Houston-based nonprofit that runs everything from charter schools to senior centers in sixty Texas counties. "We're not having mass roundups because the government can't afford it, but the randomness with which ICE is enforcing things, the chaotic nature of it, is creating a lot of fear in the immigrant community." (Because many of the people it deals with are immigrants, Baker Ripley is often referred to as the Ellis Island of Texas, and it has developed broad insight into the immigrant communities in the state.[6]) Since 2016, the group has seen a surge in calls to its hotline from immigrants worried that ICE was coming after them, Campbell said.

It wasn't just school children who were coming to blows on the playground. Immigration sparked an altercation on the floor of the Texas House of Representatives in 2017. On the penultimate day of the session, lawmakers debated Senate Bill 4 outlawing "sanctuary cities" for sixteen contentious hours. Some of the largest cities in Texas, including Houston, had refused to allow ICE to use local police, jails, and other resources for enforcing federal immigration laws. The bill sought to overturn the status quo by giving local police the right to ask anybody about their immigration status during routine traffic stops or other interactions. It also required local officials to cooperate with federal requests to detain anyone suspected of being in the country illegally. Local law enforcement officers could be fined or removed from office if they failed to comply. Democrats opposed the measure, but the bill was passed by the Republican majority.

The next day, protesters wearing red shirts filed into the gallery above the House floor and began chanting "here to stay!" Several held posters identifying themselves as illegal immigrants. Two Latino representatives, Ramon Romero and Cesar Blanco, both Democrats, turned and waved at the crowd as security escorted protesters from the gallery. Matt Rinaldi, a Republican representative from the Dallas suburb of Irving and a staunch supporter of the bill, walked over to Romero and Blanco on the House floor and told them he had called ICE to report the protesters, most of whom were Latino.

A shoving match erupted. Rinaldi claimed another Democrat, Poncho Nevarez, threatened to "get me on the way to my car." Rinaldi responded by saying that if Nevarez attempted to make good on the threat, "I would shoot him in self-defense." Rinaldi then asked for the Department of Public Safety to assign a security detail to him for protection. In a prepared statement, Rinaldi said he felt his Democratic colleagues were "inciting" the protesters, whom, he claimed, "are illegal."[7]

The tone of the immigration debate was becoming more acrimonious at the national level, too. Two Republican U.S. senators, Tom Cotton of Arkansas and David Perdue of Georgia, introduced a bill in February 2017 that would cut in half the number of green cards issued, reducing *legal* immigration by 50 percent. About a million immigrants are granted permanent residence each year. About two-thirds of them are immediate relatives of American citizens. The bill—known as the RAISE Act, for Reforming American Immigration for Strong Employment—would eliminate family-sponsorship except for spouses and minor children of citizens.[8] "Since 1965, our immigration system has been based on family reunification," immigration attorney Charles Foster said. The RAISE Act would disqualify parents of U.S. citizens for legal status, which Foster said hits close to home. "My wife's from China," he said. "She became a citizen, and we brought over her parents to help when my wife had her first baby and they never left. It's been a blessing for our family." The RAISE Act would tighten immigration policy that's been in place for more than half a century.[9]

The bill didn't pass in the spring, and Cotton reintroduced it in August.[10] President Trump supported it both times, and although the re-introduced bill was referred to the Senate Judiciary Committee, no co-sponsors signed on and the bill didn't make it out of committee.[11]

If the RAISE bill had passed, the cuts to legal immigration would have curtailed the country's economic growth and summarily eliminated the applications of about four million people who have been waiting for legal status for years.

Just after Labor Day in 2017, Trump took aim at another key provision of immigration policy: the Deferred Action for Childhood Arrivals, or DACA. Trump's predecessor, Barack Obama, had created the program by executive order in 2012. It gave two-year work and residency permits to undocumented immigrants under the age of thirty-one, primarily those who had been brought here by their parents illegally as children. To qualify, applicants had to have no criminal record, to be either enrolled in or to have graduated from high school or college, or to have been honorably discharged from the armed services. They had to pay four hundred ninety-five dollars for each permit and provide a large amount of personal information. In the five years it was in force, the program brought about eight hundred thousand young immigrants out of the shadows and allowed them to live, work, and go to college without fear of deportation.

Trump ended the program on September 5, 2017, fulfilling a campaign promise. His attorney general, Jeff Sessions, a staunch DACA opponent, made the announcement, saying that the program "denied jobs to hundreds of thousands of Americans by allowing those same jobs to go to illegal aliens." Sessions gave no evidence to support the claim.

Most DACA recipients say the program has helped them get a better paying job and become financially independent. The average participant grew up in America, and most are married and have at least one child or other relative who is an American citizen.[12]

Then, as abruptly as Trump decided to end the program, he did another about-face of sorts. Imploring Congress to come up with a law to protect those covered by DACA, he cut a deal with Democratic leaders to do just that, shunning members of his own party. He also made it clear that any DACA agreement would have to include funding for a border wall. That deal, too, fell through. In discussing the provision with senators from both parties in early January 2018, Trump discovered that the legal protections would cover immigrants from Haiti and some African nations. "Why are we having all these people from shithole countries come here?" Trump asked, according to an account in the Washington Post from people who attended the meeting.[13] He went on to suggest that the U.S. should attract more people from countries like Norway. More immigrants from Asian countries would help the economy, he added.

The racial overtones of the comments set off a political firestorm and scuttled the DACA negotiations. It brought to mind Madison Grant's eugenics junk science about the "Nordic race" that was used to close the country in 1924. Democrats, determined to get a deal, blocked a routine measure to keep the government functioning and, at midnight on January 20, 2018, the government shut down. The impasse was resolved a few days later, with Republicans promising to address DACA in the coming weeks. (Congress never did pass a DACA bill. But on June 18, 2020, the U.S. Supreme Court, in a rebuke to Trump, blocked the administration's attempt to end DACA in a 5-4 decision. In the majority opinion, Chief Justice John Roberts wrote that the court based its ruling on whether the administration had provided a "reasoned explanation for its action" to rescind the program. Trump signaled he would submit new paperwork to address the court's concerns.)

Following the DACA debacle, the administration in 2018 adopted a "zero-tolerance" policy that led to the separation of thousands of children from their parents after they were either caught entering the country illegally or turned themselves in at ports of entry seeking asylum.

Stan and others looking for a reasonable solution to illegal immigration found the rhetoric, posturing, and gamesmanship infuriating. In the age of Trump, any politician supporting a path to legal status for undocumented workers already in the country seemed to be committing political suicide.

"With all that is going on at the border the problem gets bigger and bigger," Stan said. "Smuggling of drugs, human trafficking, and rampant crime along our southern border cannot be solved unless we find a way to ID the eleven million plus undocumented already in the U.S. They are afraid to go to authorities to report the activities in their neighborhoods and that creates a sanctuary for the bad guys."

The immigration arguments that raged in 2017 and 2018 were strikingly similar to the verbal attacks that marked other periods of backlash against immigrants. What's lost amid the vitriol goes deeper than the economic benefits of immigration: The shared values that draw many immigrants to America in the first place are under siege. Many working-class whites and undocumented immigrants share a Christian faith, a belief in the strength of families, and an appreciation for the value of hard work, says Jose Garza, executive director of the Austin, Texas-based non-profit Workers Defense Project. In simple terms, they all believe in the promise of the American Dream. "That's why immigrants risk so much to come here," Garza says.

For workers like Hector, who'd started his own company after his undocumented status forced Stan to let him go, Trump's rise has brought a growing fear of deportation to a country he barely remembers from childhood. All four of his children are American citizens, and none wants to leave. His oldest daughter is preparing to enter college with plans to become a nurse. His son wants to be an architect. Returning to Mexico would scuttle their dreams. His two younger children are frightened by the prospect of living in Mexico, a country they've never seen.

The president's strident anti-immigrant comments served to make a wall largely unnecessary. As American antipathy toward immigrants has grown, illegal border crossings have declined. Even before Trump took office, the flow of illegal immigrants was reversing, thanks to the slow recovery from the Great Recession.

From 2009 through 2014, one hundred forty thousand more immigrants returned to Mexico than crossed into the United States. The flow of undocumented immigrants has continued to flag, hitting its lowest level since the early 1990s.[14] The declines continued through the first six months of Trump's presidency and beyond. Trump was building his wall, not out of steel and stone, but out of rhetoric and intimidation.

11

A Better Way

The more Stan delved into the complexity of immigration reform, the more he became convinced that his industry—and especially the drywall business—was killing its own future. Construction in Texas and many other states had become dependent on an un-documented workforce. Stan was concerned on two levels—as an employer and as a humanitarian. Despite his conflict with his father when Stan was a young man, the two had become close over the years. As he grew older, Stan began to understand his father's obsession with hard work and his fear of losing everything he'd striven to build. He also had come to admire Ralph's commitment to giving back and, long ago, had begun to emulate it. Thanks to Ralph's decades of hard work, Stan didn't have to grow up in a dirt-floor shack or build his own home from recycled wood. With age and hindsight, he understood his father's motivations. Ralph and his brothers had built one of the largest and most success-ful specialty subcontractors in the Southwest, yet if you'd asked

Ralph what he wanted to be remembered for, he would say "the work I've done to help the poor." Over the years, the Marek family has given millions of dollars to the St. Vincent DePaul Society, the Catholic outreach organization that provides food and other necessities for individuals and families living in poverty. Stan grew up seeing the dedication his father and uncles had to the poor as well as to Marek employees, and those views shaped his own.

Stan's fight to reform immigration policy "is really a moral issue," said Joseph Fiorenza, the archbishop emeritus of Galveston-Houston and the Marek family's parish priest, who has known Stan since birth. "Stan's point is: Not only is [current policy] hurting the construction business and the people who are trying to do it lawfully, it's hurting our overall economy."

Immigrants, whether legal or illegal, generally want the same thing, Fiorenza said: The chance to work to provide for their families and build better lives. But laws and current practices in the construction industry circumvent many worker protections.

Marek and other companies find themselves at a competitive disadvantage because they resist misclassification of contractors and the use of labor brokers who rely on a shadow economy of illegal immigration. One morning in the summer of 2016, Stan's phone rang, and his secretary told him a local developer was on the line. He grabbed the receiver and leaned back in his chair, propping his left foot on the credenza behind his desk and staring out the window. On the other end of the line, a developer he'd known for years began the verbal dance of contract negotiation. Stan already knew the steps, and he knew where the conversation was going. Under the leadership of Stan and his cousins, Bruce and Paul, the Marek company had grown to employ two thousand people. As its chief executive, Stan didn't typically negotiate contracts personally. But in the past few years, as potential clients often questioned the company's higher costs, more and more deals required his direct involvement. This one was no different. Marek's estimators had resisted the developer's attempts to extract a lower bid for the project, and now the developer was appealing directly to Stan. The project was significant—about twenty million dollars for drywall work in an office high rise—and the man said that, as much as he'd like to hire Marek, others would do the job for less.

Stan waited patiently. Finally, he began to tell the story of how his father had taught him that employees were the soul of the company and how Marek had a long history of trying to treat its workers right. The developer already knew the company's background, of course. Few in the construction and real estate business in Houston, or for that matter, the Southwest, didn't know Marek's reputation. "What you're getting with us," Stan said, "is someone who's doing the right thing. All our workers are trained. They all get benefits. We pay them overtime, and they pay taxes. It's not just about the low bid, it's about doing things right."

Marek ultimately won the job, but Stan had had similar conversations more often than he cared to remember. His only competitive edge these days seemed to be his reputation and an appeal to conscience. Sometimes it worked. But as oil prices began falling in late 2014, Houston's economy slowed, and competition intensified. Stan found that for many customers, cost increasingly overrode conscience. He understood. He had faced it himself—his own crisis of faith. A few years earlier, he needed a fence repaired in his backyard. He got a bid from a contractor he'd used before who paid employees overtime and benefits. Although the bid seemed fine, Stan decided to get a second one. It came in 25 percent lower. He knew why. The fencing company was using contract labor. To his surprise, Stan found his initial reaction was to take the cheaper bid. "I had to consciously say to myself, 'no that's not right,'" Stan said. "You can rationalize—'he doesn't have as much overhead, the other guy's trying to take advantage of me.' You can play that game. This is the dilemma that people have."

Stan decided to go with his regular contractor and pay more, but how many people would? While Americans are willing to pay a premium for brand status—Apple iPhones, Starbucks coffee, Yeti coolers—many just as easily skimp when it comes to workers who do manual labor for them.

A low-bid mentality permeates many businesses, but few are more trapped by it than construction. Most building is done on a budget. If the builder is a government or a non-profit, they may be required to take the lowest bid. The drive to reduce costs has, in all likelihood, spawned abuses. And if workers are undocumented, they are less likely to challenge illegal work practices for fear of being deported, fired, or both.

By turning a blind eye to workers' plights, many of Stan's competitors could offer lower bids. But Stan declined to change his policies. He refused to give in to the economic pressures that he believed were destroying the construction industry. As Stan saw it, employment was a two-way bargain between the company and its workers that, if done right, was mutually beneficial. "They know that they have a future here," Saied Alavi, Marek's operations director, said of the company's workers. "They are not here for one day or two days, so they can plan their life. They can plan their children's future. They know that they have a place to go and work, and they know that they are not going to get cheated."

If the United States doesn't reform its immigration policy, the construction business faces an unsustainable future: Workers—legal or illegal—will become harder to find. "We're not going to see the same numbers of immigrants coming in, and we're not seeing any high school kids going into the trades," Stan said. "It's hard work, it's outside work, and our kids, the millennials, are not into that. But demand for workers isn't going down, especially in growing cities."

Stan has spent years warning politicians, government bureaucrats, and his industry counterparts of the dangers. His pleas get lost amid the construction industry's focus on cost. Simply put, whoever offers the lowest bid usually gets the job, and Stan knows that by sticking to his principles he's probably losing work.

"I think sometimes he feels he's a lonely voice, but I try to tell him not to get discouraged," said Fiorenza, the priest who is also a longtime advocate for immigrants' rights. "It's a tough, tough struggle, but it's the right thing to do, and it impacts the lives of so many people."

Stan took a key step toward protecting workers by spearheading the founding of the Construction Career Collaborative, or C3, with like-minded Houston-area construction companies. The group voluntarily adopted stricter workplace safety and employment standards for its employees and promotes training. It encourages building owners to hire only contractors who issue W-2 tax forms for employees, pay overtime, and provide workers' comp coverage and safety training.

Stan believes the voluntary program will be more effective than forcing contractors to change through tighter regulations. "I don't think anybody wants to rely on the government alone," he said. "It would be so much better if we as a construction community built our labor force the way that we used to build it."

That means agreeing to pay workers well enough that they can provide for their families, offering benefits and retirement savings, and providing a chance for promotion. In other words, offering a career rather than just a job. The organization works on three principles: improving safety, providing craft training, and supporting the financial health and well-being of the craft worker.

Stan and the other founders conceived C3 with a goal of improving current working conditions. But it also focuses on training in the commercial construction industry. C3's biggest challenge, says Executive Director Chuck Gremillion, is changing contractors' view that concentrating exclusively on the lowest bid guarantees they will win the business. Instead, they should consider that low bids mean low wages and a short-term focus that makes construction jobs less appealing to young workers. "Today, the industry has a hard time attracting kids coming out of high school," Gremillion said. "You've got a craft workforce that's not as desirable [to them] because the career path is going away." While it's difficult to change attitudes, C3 has signed up more than two hundred employers to follow its principles. Large developers like Hines, the global real estate firm, and major local building owners including those of the University of Texas's M.D. Anderson Cancer Center and some big area hospitals support the program. C3 tries to avoid political controversy by staying out of immigration issues. Instead, it focuses on improving working conditions on the job site, providing training for the building trades, and rebuilding the American middle class. "We are here to train the workforce we have, regardless of where they come from," Gremillion said.

Gremillion maintains that C3 standards produce better quality work, enabling contractors to pay higher wages and benefits to attract younger workers. "If we provide craft training linked to a career path, we're going to start attracting kids," Gremillion said. "When you train people how to work skillfully, you're teaching them to create demand for their services, which, through the economic law of supply and demand, naturally grows wages."

The building owners of the M.D. Anderson Cancer Center and Texas Children's Hospital were first to agree to follow C3 guidelines. The facilities are based in the Texas Medical Center, a giant complex of research hospitals near downtown Houston. Many of the same people who approve construction designs for the center's hospitals also oversee maintenance programs. This overlap gave C3 a unique opportunity. C3 leaders convinced the building owners that paying a little more for better construction would reduce maintenance costs over the life of the building.

C3 audits projects to ensure members are complying with its standards. So far, it has found few violations, Gremillion said.

To encourage more building owners to support C3 standards, the organization must first help them understand the long-term benefits of paying higher wages and offering an improved work environment, said Jerry Nevlud, a former Marek employee. Nevlud now runs the Houston chapter of the Associated General Contractors of America, which supports the C3 initiative. By investing in better building practices, owners get higher quality work, which ultimately reduces maintenance costs, he says. Owners are "so fixated on capital costs, they don't realize what it may cost them down the line," Nevlud said. "Remember, the building's got to last sixty years or more."

While C3 has stayed out of overt immigration issues, it does seek to combat the pervasive problems facing undocumented workers in construction—wage theft, misclassification of employment status, and a lack of workers' compensation insurance.

"You've got some owners who are enlightened, and they realize that with better-trained people, long-term productivity goes up, and latent defects go down," Stan said. "Productivity has gone way down over the past twenty-five years," he stressed. "The industry's paying the same wages and the productivity's half of what it was. We're having more accidents, which impacts workers and their families. Unfortunately, some owners don't care about the social consequences or the industry's longevity. They want price. But it's really a choice: either you want price, or you want a safe job."

C3 can't fix the immigration problem, of course. Nor is it trying to. Only the government can accomplish wide-ranging reform. But C3 and its counterparts are improving the conditions for all workers, and in doing so, are helping to lay the groundwork for change.

Stan is embracing diverse approaches in his quest to infuse the construction industry with greater accountability and longevity. Marek recently began participating in an internship program with Houston-area high schools and the local community college. Students enter as high school juniors and receive hands-on training at the college. Then they intern with Marek one summer and return for their senior year in high school. When they graduate, they receive a college certificate in construction as well as a high school diploma, and their college-level credits can count toward an associate degree. Twenty-four juniors enrolled in the initial program, which started in the fall of 2019. "We went to the schools with the highest dropout rate according to the counselors," Stan said. "In their opinion most of these kids would never finish high school. Most would drop out to support their families. In some cases the thirteen dollars an hour was more than either of their parents were making."

The goal dovetails with C3's: Improve the training and the quality of the workforce and showcase a career path that young people might not have considered otherwise. "Having that employer commitment is key," said Sabra Phillips, Marek's director of talent development. "The reason it works is that it's tied to a job."

– – – –

For decades, the United States has ignored, at best, or endorsed, at worst, an immigration system that is not working. There's a disconnect between the nation's economic need for imported workers and policies that restrict the supply of those workers. In the simplest terms, these are the two main forces at the heart of today's illegal immigration problem.

Many business owners already understand the need for immigrant labor. They support a system that shields undocumented workers from deportation, improves the identification process, and brings these workers out of the shadow economy and onto the public tax rolls. Many of the native-born workers hired by these employers strongly disagree. It will take more than rhetoric on both sides to reach consensus on immigration's economic impact. "Explaining why comprehensive immigration reform is good for business is not the same as explaining why it's good for working people," said Jose Garza with the Workers Defense Project. "It's a lot more complicated than saying 'illegals are taking your jobs.' How do you get the ranch hand in West Texas to see their story in the story of the undocumented?"

One way to proceed is to make clear that when the undocumented are paid less than they deserve, native-born workers also see their pay scales reduced. Consumers face a similar choice when they pay more for food that's produced humanely, such as cage-free eggs, or when they choose homes built to higher energy-efficient standards. The same consideration should apply to buildings constructed by workers who are treated fairly. "There's a monetary, economic, and business value in cage-free eggs," Garza said. "I believe there's an absolute value in cage-free workers."

Instead, workers remain trapped in a broken immigration system with too few incentives to fix it. Most of the cost of illegal immigration falls on state and local governments in terms of healthcare, education, and law enforcement, so federal lawmakers have little economic incentive to change things. And native-born Americans have never experienced the complexity, unfairness, and danger of the immigration process, so they're prone to adopt ill-informed conclusions or platitudes such as "what part of illegal don't you understand?" Those who think illegal immigration can be solved without changing current policies are left with two choices: "You can either deport everybody, or you can continue to ignore it, which is what we've been doing since 1986," said Norman Adams, the TxSIP director. "We've basically had de facto amnesty since 1986." That system hasn't worked well for anybody except, perhaps, the labor brokers.

Any solution must increase the cost of illegal entry and decrease the cost of legal entry, Adams said. Yet for decades, U.S. immigration policy has focused almost exclusively on boosting the cost of illegal entry through stricter security measures with little regard for making it easier to enter the country legally. Until governments and businesses address that divide, a solution is unlikely. "We have a system where many people who desire to come to the United States for work in many cases don't have a pathway to come here, they don't have a line they can get in," said Jawetz of the Center for American Progress.

By mid-2018, things seemed to be moving even further from a solution. With the RAISE Act designed to curtail family sponsorships for would-be immigrants dead in committee, the Trump administration took matters into its own hands. It stepped up efforts to reduce not just illegal immigration, but legal immigration as well. Between the 2016 and 2019 fiscal years, the government issued 25 percent fewer visas. The administration's actions also were expected to reduce by 30 percent the number of legal immigrants receiving permanent residence each year.[1]

– – – –

Stan struggles with the toll of illegal immigration every day. He sees the damage done to workers—from low wages to little or no safety training. And he lives with the blows to his industry—from declining quality to a race to the bottom on pricing. The story of today's illegal immigrant contrasts with his own family history. The Marek journey is a tale of the American Dream fulfilled by immigrants and their children who rose from a dirt-floor cabin to run a major company. "Many in our industry are taking the easy way out by adopting non-employee business models instead of committing to building a labor force," Stan says. "And to me, that's not right."

Stan's children haven't joined the family business, but he hopes one day they will. Stan and his cousins, Bruce and Paul, want to leave a company that represents the values instilled by their elders, John, Bill, and Ralph. "It's about doing the right things," Stan said. "None of us would be proud of a labor-intensive company without employees. The workers are the fabric of the company, and without them, what would we have?"

12

Stan's Plan

The rains began falling on Houston on August 25, 2017. Further down the coast, near Corpus Christi, a major hurricane with sustained winds of one hundred twenty miles an hour slammed ashore. Houston had endured its share of hurricanes and tropical storms, but Hurricane Harvey was different. The storm didn't leave. For five days, Harvey wobbled around central Texas, and its outer rain bands never departed from Houston's skies. The killer storm unleashed thirty-four trillion gallons of rainfall, more than any storm in U.S. history. One part of the city got almost fifty-two inches, and the average for the area—roughly the size of New Jersey—was more than forty inches.

Houston was built on a flat, coastal plain intercut with bayous. As the deluge persisted, those bayous began to rise. Streets flooded, then yards flooded, and eventually, tens of thousands of homes flooded. When the waters finally receded, Houston faced an unprecedented crisis.

Within days, damage estimates exceeded one hundred ninety billion dollars, making Harvey by far the costliest storm ever—more than the expense of Hurricane Katrina and Superstorm Sandy combined. AccuWeather estimated the destruction would shave 1 percent from the country's gross domestic product.

Parts of Houston remained uninhabitable for months. Tens of thousands of homes across the state were destroyed and hundreds of thousands sustained some sort of damage. Even before the skies cleared, Houston, a city known for its resilience, began talking about how it would rebuild.

"Harvey can be characterized as the largest housing disaster in the U.S.," said Marvin Odum, the former Shell Oil president who served as Houston's chief recovery officer. In all, an estimated three hundred thousand homes were damaged or destroyed, creating a need for labor to rebuild on a massive scale.

For Stan Marek, the question wasn't how, but who. With the construction industry already struggling under a labor shortage, who would do the work of rebuilding Houston and the Texas Gulf Coast? With the passage of the state law banning sanctuary cities just months before the storm hit, the construction industry in Houston already was seeing its workforce decline. Many Latinos, both documented and undocumented, fled Texas amid growing concern that local police would start rounding up immigrants.

The state was scaring away the very workers Houston and other coastal cities battered by Harvey required to rebuild. Restoration of the Gulf Coast, Stan knew, would depend on an alternative to deportations, walls, and hateful rhetoric. It would need to draw on the large number of undocumented workers already in the city and the state.

"We need to find a way to bring those people out of the shadows, to allow them to work and to pay taxes, while they work on coming to some position of legal status," Odum said. "When you try to recover from something like Harvey, over a period of the next several years, that's an enormous surge of activity. As far as I'm concerned, we need all hands on deck."

Stan recalled the response to Tropical Storm Allison, the closest thing in modern history to Harvey that Houston had seen. That storm had dumped twenty-seven inches of rain on Houston in twenty-four hours in 2001, causing nine billion dollars in damage. Thousands of workers, many undocumented, flocked to the city to help with the rebuilding. Their efforts were welcomed, with few questions asked about their immigration status.

Sixteen years later, however, Texas was far less accommodating to the undocumented, even in the state's time of need. While the sanctuary cities ban had been temporarily blocked by the courts in late summer of 2017, the sentiment was clear: undocumented workers weren't welcome.

"I need a legal way to be able to access that workforce," Odum said. That didn't mean giving all workers blanket legal status, but at least giving them temporary status so they could work legally without fear of deportation.

As Texas struggled to find recruits for the rebuilding effort, construction demand was rising in other states. Workers in other cities had less reason to come to Houston to help with rebuilding, especially since in many states, wages are higher than they are in Texas.

Stan viewed the Harvey recovery, with its need for additional construction workers, as an opportunity to change the tone of the immigration debate. In a guest column for the Houston Chronicle in September 2017, he called for granting the six hundred thousand undocumented workers in Houston some type of legal status immediately. Other local business leaders supported his "ID and Tax" plan, calling for workers to be identified and put on company payrolls where their wages would be taxed as required of all full-time employees. Immigrants may have helped rebuild Houston after Allison, but many were taken advantage of by labor brokers. This time, Stan vowed, it would be different.

ID and Tax wouldn't be carte-blanche amnesty. In ex-change for legal status, immigrant workers would consent to a background check and get a tamper-proof photo ID. Once the government determined they had committed no felonies, they would work for a sponsoring employer who agreed to cover their payroll taxes and provide accident insurance. The plan was simi-lar to how current work visas already are handled.

Stan remains determined to reverse the system of exploitation and abuse that holds back immigrants and hurts his industry. He seeks a rational policy that will bring the country's more than eleven million undocumented immigrants out of the shadows and into the mainstream economy. Stan reiterates the logic behind his thinking every chance he gets. These immigrants cannot vote or receive welfare, yet they work as productive members of society. Many have been illegally in the U.S. for decades and are as much a part of the landscape as legal citizens. Americans have already invested billions of dollars in educating their children. By iden-tifying these illegal immigrants and taxing them for working in the United States, governments will add more money to public coffers, improve wages and working conditions, and ensure the workers have needed protections without fearing deportation.

If Stan has his way, immigration reform would involve sever-al key steps, starting with the DREAM Act. Since 2001, Congress has flirted with the Development, Relief, and Education for Alien Minors Act, which, like DACA, would grant conditional residency for undocumented minors. If these immigrants meet additional qualifications, the act would create the opportunity for them to achieve permanent residency. The U.S. House approved a version of the bill in 2010, but the Senate came up five votes short. Af-ter the measure failed to pass, President Obama in 2012 signed the executive order creating DACA. (DACA and the DREAM Act are similar in their intent—protecting undocumented immigrants brought to the U.S. as children from deportation—but as an executive order, DACA could be undone as Obama's successor tried to do. The DREAM Act would codify the protections as law.[1])

Stan would take the DREAM Act one step further. He would extend its provisions of conditional and eventual permanent residency not just to children, but to their five million parents. Under his proposal, undocumented adults would receive legal status for three years and a work permit giving them time to begin meeting the requirements for permanent resident status. Essentially, employers would sponsor adult DREAMers until they achieved legal status, ensuring that most of the applicants for the program had a job.

DACA and the Temporary Protected Status program, which allows workers to stay in the United States on a temporary basis for employment purposes, provide similar, if temporary, protections from deportation, allowing immigrants to remain and work in the United States. ID and Tax would take a similar approach but make those protections ongoing on a renewable basis that would be reviewed every three years.

Of course, this provision only works if the Internal Revenue Service and the Department of Labor cooperate to ensure that employers hire workers as full-time employees and deduct taxes from their paychecks, rather than classifying them as independent contractors. Currently, the two agencies share little information. By forming a joint task force to address immigration, they could increase compliance for both taxes and working conditions, giving immigrants a process for reporting violations without fearing deportation. At the same time, the measure would increase federal tax revenue.

Stan's plan requires the Department of Homeland Security to complete thorough background checks on immigrants already in the country and develop a secure, tamper-proof form of identification rather than the easily forged Social Security card. Providing an ID to every immigrant who is in the United States illegally would allow the government to know who they are and where they live. In addition, allowing them to get a driver's license would give immigrants greater mobility, helping reduce regional labor shortages without compromising security. Many illegal immigrants in Texas, for instance, are afraid to leave the state because they can't get a driver's license.

"That would be a step that brings people to conventional legal employment relationships," said Mark Erlich, with Harvard's Labor and Worklife Program. "It's a positive step for those workers, for the industry, and for taxpayers as a whole. It takes these workers out of the shadows, so that they have the rights that go along with being an employee, which include the right to a minimum wage, the right to overtime payments, the right to anti-discrimination laws, the right to form union organizations, all of those rights come along with being an employee. If you're an independent contractor, you have none of those rights. You're basically on your own."[2]

Stan's plan would direct ICE to stop auditing employers. He says the current system punishes them twice—once by forcing them to fire workers and then again when disreputable competitors hire the workers their former employers trained. The agency should instead work with the IRS to ensure that undocumented workers are properly identified and taxed.

Once those basic objectives are in place, Stan wants Congress to develop a path to legal status for all immigrants who are already in the United States. Critics call it amnesty, but deporting millions of workers who contribute to the economy would create a huge labor shortage in industries including construction. That in turn could cause escalating prices for homes, offices, and other real estate, Stan contends. Multiplied across agriculture, meat packing, and other immigrant-dominated business, the economic fallout becomes profound.

Finally, the plan requires that both U.S. borders be secured by reasonable means. He suggested neither a physical wall nor a metaphorical wall of fear and intimidation. Instead he's proposing a systematic monitoring that takes advantage of new, more afford-able technology such as drones and motion sensors. The system would identify all workers and require entry into the E-Verify sys-tem. At the same time, employers would be required to pay all employment taxes on them.

The plan represents a feasible compromise that preserves bor-der integrity while addressing the economic realities of immigra-tion and providing the millions of undocumented workers a way out of the shadows, Stan said.

With Trump's election, Stan realized he'd have to scale back be-fore he'd even had a chance to widely promote the plan he still be-lieves in. The president had been in office only seven months when Harvey struck and Houston clamored to rebuild, but Trump's an-ti-immigrant rhetoric had poisoned the chance for rational debate, let alone adoption of Stan's sweeping immigration proposals. By late 2017, Stan worried that any plan creating the possibility for millions of undocumented workers to become citizens would de-rail any attempts at reform. Instead, he regrouped around two cru-cial and specific tenets of his initiative: "ID and Tax."

These provisions would identify undocumented immigrants already in the country and create a legal protection for them to work, ensuring that they pay taxes. The initiative would reduce many of the abuses endured by immigrant workers and allow them to work and remain in the country without fear of deporta-tion. Because the government would have their personal informa-tion on file, security concerns would be reduced as well.

"If they've been here more than five years, they get an ID, and they get entered in the E-Verify system," Stan said. "Then they go to work for an employer who puts them on the payroll and pays taxes. If employers don't comply, the workers have recourse in the courts or with the government."

Those provisions alone, Stan argues, would change the nature of the immigration debate. His program would remove employers' excuses that paying undocumented workers overtime and benefits would be too expensive and cause companies to lose projects. If all employers faced the same requirements, the competitive landscape would be more level than it is now, Stan argues. He has a project in mind for testing his system: "If Trump is serious about building a wall, then let's take the workers who are here, ID them, and let them build the wall." He was only half joking.

Distrust would undoubtedly linger, but by providing a path to legal status, undocumented workers already in the U.S. would be able to secure a driver's license, open a bank account, and participate openly in their communities. Law enforcement could again rely on immigrant neighborhoods to help with community policing and doctors and nurses would have access to reliable medical records on the immigrant patients they were treating. Immigrant parents would no longer fear being arrested by ICE agents if they show up at their children's schools.

"Employers like myself would find the employees we need to rebuild this city—not with the labor that will be exploited because of immigration status, but with legal workers paying taxes and protected with insurance," Stan wrote in the Chronicle in the fall of 2017.

It wasn't the full-scale reform that Stan had long yearned for, but it would be a good first step. Without the help of illegal immigrants, Texas's recovery would likely be painful and protracted.

Houston is a city eager to embrace its rebirth and its long history of welcoming immigrants could represent a turning point. As the 2020 hurricane season dawned, a reporter called Stan and asked him if the city had the workforce it needed to recover from another major storm. Stan's answer was immediate: No. Not even close. The rebuilding effort from Harvey was still dragging on because of labor shortages the last time. Stan, however, continues to hope that Houston's inclusiveness and vibrant immigrant community will seed a solution to America's long-deficient immigration policies. And with those advantages—bolstered by rational debate and thoughtful action—might also come hope for the future of the construction industry. It's a goal to which Stan Marek, like his father before him, has devoted his life.

Epilogue

As the COVID-19 outbreak spread across the United States in the first half of 2020, healthcare workers found themselves on the front lines of efforts to stop the pandemic's advance. One in six of those workers was an immigrant, including almost 29 percent of physicians, a study by the New American Economy found.

Immigrants work in even higher concentrations in other segments of medicine—comprising almost 37 percent of home healthcare workers, for example. "In the areas where it is most critical, immigrants are playing even greater roles—serving as the first person you might see at the hospital intake, to nurses, to the doctors themselves," said Andrew Lim, NAE's director of quantitative research.

NAE estimates that some forty-five thousand healthcare workers in the United States are undocumented, most of them serving in supporting roles such as aides, laundry personnel, and food preparers. Another sixty-two thousand are DACA recipients. As virus infections surged across the country, many of those DACA workers were waiting to see if the U.S. Supreme Court would uphold the Trump administration's executive order to eliminate their protections, leaving them vulnerable to deportation.

"To remove healthcare workers at this critical moment in time, as healthcare needs are immense, seems to not make sense," Lim said. Fortunately, that didn't happen, although Trump's promise to rescind DACA anew still casts doubt over the workers' future.

For the undocumented, working in healthcare poses a dual risk: daily potential exposure to deadly viruses and other diseases and a lack of access to medical treatment if they get sick.[1] The workers themselves are in danger, of course, but their situation also creates a broader peril in public health. Workers who may be infected and show up for work anyway, out of fear of losing pay or jobs, could spread the virus to others.

The pandemic brought to light the critical roles that immigrants play in the U.S. economy. They're active in services from cleaning, to deliveries, to food preparation and supply. In the orchards of California and the fields of South Texas, agricultural workers found themselves carrying letters from their employers declaring them "essential" after the Department of Homeland Security deemed that field workers were "critical to the food supply chain."

"It's like suddenly they realized we are here contributing," forty-three-year-old Nancy Silva, an undocumented immigrant from Mexico, told the New York Times. Silva, who was working in the clementine groves south of Bakersfield, California, lives with the constant threat of deportation. The letter eased her fears, but it didn't eliminate them.[2] Like thousands of other migrant agriculture workers, she is caught between the reality of America's economic needs and the irrational vitriol of its politics. She is both essential and unwanted at the same time.

Meat packers rely on immigrant labor. As much as 50 percent of the industry's workforce is made up of undocumented workers from Mexico, Guatemala, El Salvador, and East African nations.[3] As the pandemic spread across the country, the U.S. Centers for Disease Control found that 3 percent of workers in more than a hundred processing plants tested positive for COVID-19 in April 2020. That number may be low because of limited testing, CDC researchers said. Because workers in meat plants must do their jobs in close conditions and can't distance themselves from each other, the virus has advanced more rapidly through their ranks.[4]

As workers got sick—and at least twenty died—meatpackers faced shutdowns that threatened to create shortages in supermarkets nationwide. President Trump invoked the Defense Production Act to classify meat producers as critical infrastructure to keep the processing plants running. The industry, which like construction faced a shortage of workers before the pandemic, has raised pay and offered bonuses to healthy workers. But as more in their ranks showed symptoms of the virus, requiring a fourteen-day self-quarantine, labor shortages loomed, and the meat supply chain remained under pressure.[5]

Further up that chain, farmers, ranchers. and other food suppliers that rely on immigrants to stay afloat have struggled as well. With restaurants and schools closed, many farmers couldn't find markets for their goods. Some had to destroy crops. In Washington state, farmers amassed a one-billion-pound surplus of potatoes. Dairy farmers, already facing lower prices before the pandemic, were hit hard by declining demand, dumping as much as 3.7 million gallons of milk a day, according to the Dairy Farmers of America. Chicken processors, meanwhile, had to euthanize tens of thousands of birds because of reduced capacity at processing plants.[6]

By early April 2020, Dallas restaurateur Jim Baron had closed his four Tex-Mex locations and laid off most of his workforce. He still kept a little money coming in with take-out service, but in the first week of the month, his revenue was just twenty-five thousand dollars, a plunge from two hundred seventy-five thousand dollars for the same week in 2019. Restaurants use current revenue to pay past obligations, so when the revenue nosedived, Baron struggled to pay vendors for deliveries they'd already made and employees for work they'd already done. "It's a very difficult time," he said. "And it's the reality facing every restaurant in the United States."

Like the struggling meatpackers, farmers, and ranchers, Baron had many employees who were immigrants living paycheck to paycheck. Forced to lay them off, he worried that many wouldn't return to the restaurant business when the economy recovers because they would find work elsewhere. Multiplied across other industries, the loss of jobs and businesses is likely to be devastating to America's attempt to rebuild its economy. "They're really a huge contributing member of the system, and we're going to lose that economic value," Baron said of immigrant workers. "Once the smoke clears on this crisis, we're going to have to rebuild, and we're going to need [immigrants] and their work is going to be appreciated. I think they have a chance, you know, of being seen differently by the average American."[7]

The 2020 Covid-19 pandemic threw economic assumptions into chaos. Pessimists wonder how the United States will deal with unemployment levels that by late May approached 15 percent—the highest since the Great Depression. Will more than twenty million desperate out-of-work Americans finally accept the menial jobs they just months earlier renounced? Will those jobs even exist as businesses fail? President Trump has already barred both legal and illegal immigrants from entering the country during the pandemic. Will he extend those restrictions and for how long? With the U.S. suffering the most cases and deaths in the global health crisis, will anyone want to come here to work if they could? Will there be better opportunities elsewhere?

"The pandemic has definitely created uncertainty," Stan said. "But I feel like construction will rebound quickly. There is just so much demand for roads, buildings, houses, and so forth. I do think that immigration will be restricted, and we must find a way to encourage young men and women in our high schools to enter the trades. I doubt many will want to work in a job that offers no training, no benefits, no career. And I think they want to be tax-paying citizens and contribute to a better society. Fixing this broken immigration system, especially dealing in a humane way with the eleven million already here, would be a great start."

In early 2020, construction workers were designated as essential workers. Stan Marek sees a correlation between the aftermath of Hurricane Harvey and the rebuilding effort to recover from COVID-19. Like Baron, he believes immigrants will be vital.

"Those of us who lived through Hurricane Harvey should remember who participated in the cleanup and rebuild of our city—mucking out houses, tearing out wet sheetrock, hauling off trash, and other 'dirty jobs' that no one else wanted to do," he said. "Where would we have been without these essential workers? Now more than ever we must get serious about building a resilient workforce for the next disaster. Ignoring the fact that we have hundreds of thousands of workers in the shadows that we are relying on in time of crisis makes no sense."

The Rational Middle

Stan's fight for sensible immigration reform is far from over. He continues to explore every avenue for increasing public understanding of the issues and to bolster political willpower for immigration reform. Over the years, he has tried many tactics, including political fund raisers for candidates who pledged support and giving talks around the country on the benefits for reform. Nothing has changed attitudes significantly. Stan and his team believe a social media platform is a tool that might make a difference because it can reach millions in a productive, powerful way.

In 2017, he began working with business leaders to raise money for a YouTube video series called "The Rational Middle of Immigration." The eight- to eleven-minute films, each on a different topic of the immigration debate, explore the challenges facing the country through the eyes of immigrants, municipalities, business owners, and citizens on the ground who find themselves confronting illegal immigration.

Developed by acclaimed independent filmmaker Gregory Kallenberg, the series aims to educate and empower voters on immigration issues and provide cover for elected officials. It is

a way to shape sensible policy solutions and create a deeper understanding of complex immigration issues. The Rational Middle
cuts through rhetoric and helps people understand the facts surrounding those issues. Ultimately, the initiative hopes to develop
common ground in the immigration debate.

Working with the Center for Houston's Future and the Mexico
Center at Rice University's James A. Baker III Institute for Public
Policy, the Rational Middle released ten videos by the fall of 2019.
More are in production. "Through the films, social media messag-
ing, and public events, we can open a path for the public at large
to have a civil discussion and consider solutions," Kallenberg said.
To supplement and enhance the videos, a weekly podcast delves
into more detail on certain immigration topics and offers insights
from experts on the latest immigration news.

To see the films and listen to the podcast, visit
rationalmiddle.com/immigration. To schedule a Rational Middle
event for your group, go to *rationalmiddle.com/events/.*

Acknowledgments

Stan Marek and I first talked about writing a book on immigration reform in the early summer of 2016. Since then we've had a lot of discussions about how we should approach the book and what it should say. He was uncomfortable being the focus of the narrative, but I was drawn to the story of a company founded by the grandchildren of immigrants wrestling with the struggle that illegal immigration poses for that company.

Stan loves books. The first few times we met, he shoved a book into my hand and recommended that I read up on topics ranging from construction to self-improvement. His belief in the importance of books—which, sadly, is increasingly rare these days—helped give this project life.

I'm indebted to Stan's colleagues, Mike Holland, Larry Williams, Saied Alavi, and Jorge Rodriguez for sharing their time, stories, and insights as I researched this project. In addition, Stan's associates in the industry, Jim Stevenson, Jerry Nevlud, Tom Vaughn, Pat Kiley, and Chuck Gremillion all helped educate me about the construction industry, the impact of illegal immigration, and the crisis facing craft work. Norman Adams, the executive director of TxSIP, provided valuable insights into that organization's efforts.

Richard Shaw spent hours on the phone explaining union history and organized labor's views on the immigrant workforce. Jose Garza with the Worker Defense Project took time to share his insights and allowed me to attend a WDP meeting in Austin, Texas. Julia Kranzthor graciously served as my translator.

Hector was willing to share his story, even though he is undocumented and fears deportation, with one condition: I could not use his last name. Other members of the undocumented community related their stories but asked to keep their identities secret.

Steve Klineberg took time away from his own book project to talk about his research on immigration and Houston's shifting demographics. Charles Foster and Jacob Monty, both busy immigration lawyers, also found the time to help me increase my understanding of the complexity of immigration law.

Steve Etkin, with the Association of the Wall and Ceiling Industry, walked me through the issues facing the drywall business nationally.

And Stan's old parish priest, now archbishop emeritus, Joseph Fiorenza, added his view of both Stan and the immigration issue from the humanitarian perspective.

Stan's father, Ralph Marek, who died in April 2020 at age 95, allowed me to visit him in his home while he was recuperating from a bout of pneumonia so I could capture his first-hand knowledge of Marek's early days.

My colleagues at 30 Point Strategies, especially Genevieve Rozansky, Adam Levy, Andrew Thrasher, Micah Ezekiel, and Kim Keller were invaluable with their help and support in researching and editing this manuscript. Anton Ioukhnovets handled the design work and came up with just the right cover.

Gail Connor Roche, my editor for many years at Bloomberg News, sharpened her red pencil to make the prose read better than I ever could.

Gregory Kallenberg introduced me to the world of filmmaking, and the cross-collaboration with the Rational Middle on this project has been exhilarating.

My wife, Laura, once again a "book widow," found herself drawn to this project and gave her time to read the manuscript twice. My mother-in-law, Sue Robertson, also gave it an early read, unexpectedly, and offered her feedback as well.

—*Loren C. Steffy*

Notes

Preface

[1] "Texas Needs the Workers: An Analysis of the Economic and Fiscal Impact of Undocumented Workers," The Perryman Group, Feb 2016, 12, https://www.perrymangroup.com/media/uploads/report/perryman-texas-needs-the-workers-01-2016.pdf.

Chapter One — Firings and Ice

[1] Charles Foster interview, Feb. 10, 2017.
[2] "Texas Needs the Workers," The Perryman Group, 12.

Chapter Two — The Two Percent Solution

[1] Liz Stansfeld (ed.) *An Immigrant Family's History of Survival*, (Self-published, Houston: 1988), 6.
[2] Ibid, 5.
[3] Ibid, 25.
[4] Ibid, 25.
[5] Benjamin Franklin, *Writings*, "Letter to Peter Collinson," May 9, 1753, (Literary Classics of the United States, New York: 1987) 472.
[6] Franklin, *Writings*, "Observations Concerning the Increase of Mankind, People of Countries, etc." 374.
[7] Frances DeWitt (secretary for the commonwealth), "The Material Condition of the People of Massachusetts," Fifteenth Report to the Legislature of Massachusetts, published in *Christian Examiner*, 1858, Vol. 65, 53.
[8] "US Population From 1900," Demographia, http://www.demographia.com/db-uspop1900.htm.
[9] J.A. Lindsay (rev.) "The Passing of the Great Race, or the Racial Basis of European History," *The Eugenics Review*, July 1917, 9 (2), 139–141, https://www.ncbi.nlm.nih.gov/pmc/articles/PMC2942213/.
[10] Charles C. Alexander, "Prophet of American Racism: Madison Grant and the Nordic Myth," *Phylon* 1962, 23 (1), 73-90, https://www.jstor.org/stable/i212147.
[11] Lindsay, *Eugenics Review* 139–141.
[12] Tom Gjelten, *A Nation of Nations* (Simon & Schuster, New York: 2015), 85-86.
[13] "Dillingham Commission (1907-1910)" Immigration to the United States, 1789-1930, Harvard University Library Open Collections Program, http://ocp.hul.harvard.edu/immigration/dillingham.html.
[14] Alan Fram and Jonathan Lemire, "Trump: Why allow immigrants from `shithole countries'?" *The Associated Press*, Jan. 12, 2018 https://apnews.com/fdda2ff0b877416c8ae1c1a77a3cc425/Trump:-Why-allow-immigrants-from-%27shithole-countries%27.
[15] Daniel Okrent, *The Guarded Gate: Bigotry, Eugenics, and the Law That Kept Two Generations of Jews, Italians, and Other European Immigrants Out of America*, (New York: Scribner, 2019), 360-361.
[16] "National Origins Act." Laws.com, http://immigration.laws.com/national-origins-act.
[17] Patricia Bernstein, *Ten Dollars to Hate: The Texas Man Who Fought the Klan*, (Texas A&M University Press, College Station, Texas: 2017), 13.
[18] Ibid., 15.
[19] Ibid., 17-25.
[20] Gjelten, *Nation of Nations*, 89.
[21] Okrent, *The Guarded Gate*, 294-295.
[22] Congressional Record, April 9, 1924, 5961-62.
[23] "Applaud Alien Bill in D.A.R. Convention," *New York Times*, April 19, 1924.
[24] Gjelten, *Nation of Nations*, 91.
[25] Stansfeld, *Immigrant Family's History*, 25-30.

Chapter Three — Help Wanted

[1] Barbara J. Elliott and Ralph Marek, *Doing Business With the Holy Spirit*, (Self-Published, Houston: 2014), 3-4.

[2] Liz Stansfeld (ed.) *An Immigrant Family's History of Survival*, (Self published, Houston, 1988), 45; and Elliott, *Holy Spirit*, 4-5.

[3] Douglas S. Massey, Jorge Durand and Nolan J. Malone, *Beyond Smoke and Mirrors: Mexican Immigration in an Era of Economic Integration*, (Russell Sage Foundation, New York: 2002) 29, 31.

[4] Ibid., 33.

[5] Stansfeld, *Immigrant Family's History*, 45.

[6] Ibid., 50-53.

[7] Elliott, *Holy Spirit*, 7.

[8] Massey, Durand and Nolan, *Beyond Smoke and Mirrors*, 33-34.

[9] Ibid.

[10] Elliott, *Holy Spirit*, 8.

[11] Stansfeld, *Immigrant Family's History*, 60.

[12] Ibid., 56.

[13] Liz Stansfeld (ed.), *The History of the Marek Family of Companies: The First 50 Years*," (Self-published, Houston: 1988), 2.

[14] Haniya Rae, "An Exciting History of Drywall," *The Atlantic*, July 29, 2016, https://www.theatlantic.com/technology/archive/2016/07/an-exciting-history-of-drywall/493502/.

[15] Scott Gibson, "How to Hang Drywall," This Old House, https://www.thisoldhouse.com/how-to/how-to-hang-drywall.

[16] Stansfeld, *History of Marek*, 3-5.

[17] Massey, Durand and Nolan, *Beyond Smoke and Mirrors*, 35.

[18] Ibid., 36.

[19] Ibid., 36.

[20] Stephen Harrigan, *Big Wonderful Thing* (The University of Texas Press, Austin, Texas: 2019) 705-707.

[21] Ibid, 707.

[22] Ralph Marek interview, June 20, 2017.

[23] Stansfeld, *History of Marek*, 9-11.

Chapter Four — Immigration Becomes Illegal

[1] Barbara J. Elliott, Ralph Marek, *Doing Business With the Holy Spirit*, (Self-Published, Houston: 2014), 36.

[2] Liz Stansfeld (ed.), *The History of the Marek Family of Companies: The First 50 Years*," (Self-published, Houston: 1988), 13-18.

[3] Elliott, *Holy Spirit*, 41.

[4] Elliott, *Holy Spirit*, 40.

[5] Douglas S. Massey, Jorge Durand and Nolan J. Malone, *Beyond Smoke and Mirrors: Mexican Immigration in an Era of Economic Integration*, (Russell Sage Foundation, New York: 2002), 37.

[6] Ibid.

[7] Kevin Baker, "Living in LBJ's America," *The New York Times*, Aug. 28, 2016, Sunday Review, 1-4.

[8] "Depression, War, and Civil Rights: Hispanics in the Southwest," History, Art & Archives, U.S. House of Representatives, http://history.house.gov/Exhibitions-and-Publications/HAIC/Historical-Essays/Separate-Interests/Depression-War-Civil-Rights/.

[9] Massey, Durand and Nolan, *Beyond Smoke and Mirrors*, 37.

[10] Ibid., 38-39.

[11] Ibid., 41-42.

[12] Baker, "Living in LBJ's America," 5.

[13] Steve Kleinberg interview, Feb. 10, 2017.

[14] Philip E. Wolgin, "The Immigration and Nationality Act of 1965 Turns 50," Center for American Progress, Oct. 16, 2015, https://www.americanprogress.org/issues/immigration/news/2015/10/16/123477/the-immigration-and-nationality-act-of-1965-turns-50/.

[15] Massey, Durand and Nolan, *Beyond Smoke and Mirrors*, 43.

[16] Wolgin, "Immigration and Nationality Act."

[17] Tom Gjelten, *A Nation of Nations* (Simon & Schuster, New York: 2015), 138.

[18] Massey, Durand and Nolan, *Beyond Smoke and Mirrors*, 42-45.

Chapter Five — A New Era of Mexican Labor

[1] Texas State Historical Association, "Houston Ship Channel," https://tshaonline.org/handbook/online/articles/rhh11.

[2] Ralph Marek interview, June 20, 2017.

[3] Barbara J. Elliott, Ralph Marek, *Doing Business With the Holy Spirit*, (Self-Published, Houston: 2014), 101-105.

[4] Douglas S. Massey, Jorge Durand and Nolan J. Malone, *Beyond Smoke and Mirrors: Mexican Immigration in an Era of Economic Integration*, (Russell Sage Foundation, New York: 2002), 47.

[5] Ibid.

[6] Liz Stansfeld (ed.), *The History of the Marek Family of Companies: The First 50 Years*," (Self-published, Houston: 1988), 87-107.

[7] Mark Erlich interview for Rational Middle podcast, unaired, Feb. 12, 2020.

[8] "Why trade unions are declining," *The Economist*, Sept. 29, 2015, http://www.economist.com/blogs/economist-explains/2015/09/economist-explains-19.

[9] Gary M. Fink, "Labor Law Revision and the End of the Postwar Labor Accord," *Organized Labor and American Politics 1894-1994: The Labor-Liberal Alliance* (Keven Boyce, ed.) (Albany, New York: State University of New York Press, 1998), 239-241.

[10] "The Immigration Reform and Control Act: What It Is, Why It Matters," Arizona State University, http://asu.news21.com/archive/2009/the_first_immigration_amnesty/.

[11] Denise S. Smith and Robert Schlanser, "National Issues, Local Costs: The Trend Toward State and Local Control of Immigration," http://alsb.roundtablelive.org/Resources/Documents/NP%20 2008%20Smith-Schlanser.pdf.

[12] Massey, Durand and Nolan, *Beyond Smoke and Mirrors*, 49.

[13] Ibid, 49-50.

Chapter Six — Rise of the Independents

[1] Marek internal memo, 2007.

[2] United States Border Patrol, "Nationwide Illegal Alien Apprehensions Fiscal Years 1925-2018, https://www.cbp.gov/sites/default/files/assets/documents/2019-Mar/bp-total-apps-fy1925-fy2018.pdf.

[3] "Census of Housing," U.S. Census Bureau, https://www.census.gov/hhes/www/housing/census/historic/values.html.

[4] Ted Hesson, "Five Ways Immigration System Changed After 9/11," ABC News, Sept. 13, 2012, http://abcnews.go.com/ABC_Univision/News/ways-immigration-system-changed-911/story?id=17231590.

[5] "E-Verify Usage Statistics," U.S. Department of Homeland Security and USCIS, https://www.uscis.gov/e-verify/about-program/e-verify-statistics.

[6] Matt Weinberger, "The founder of identity theft prevention company Symantec bought reportedly had his identity stolen 13 times," Business Insider, Nov. 21, 2016. http://www.businessinsider.com/lifelock-symantec-ceo-identity-theft-ftc-charges-2016-11.

[7] Alexia Fernández Campbell, "The Truth About Undocumented Immigrants and Taxes," *The Atlantic*, Sept. 12, 2016, https://www.theatlantic.com/business/archive/2016/09/undocumented-immigrants-and-taxes/499604/.

[8] Amanda Sakuma, "Undocumented workers are keeping a key benefit program afloat," MSNBC, Nov. 19, 2014.

[9] Ibid.

[10] Louis Jacobson, "Medicare and Social Security: What you paid compared with what you get," PolitiFact, Feb. 1, 2013, http://www.politifact.com/truth-o-meter/article/2013/feb/01/medicare-and-social-security-what-you-paid-what-yo/.

[11] "Build a Better Texas," Workers Defense Project, 2013, http://constructioncitizen.com/sites/constructioncitizen.com/files/Build_a_Better_Texas.pdf.

Chapter Seven — A Pathway to Failure

[1] "A Guide to S.744: Understanding the 2013 Senate Immigration Bill," American Immigration Council, July 10, 2013, https://americanimmigrationcouncil.org/research/guide-s744-understanding-2013-senate-immigration-bill.

[2] Nancy Lofholm, "Fear from Swift plant raid resonates in Greeley six years later," The Denver Post, Jan. 14, 2013, http://www.denverpost.com/2013/01/14/fear-from-swift-plant-raid-resonates-in-greeley-six-years-later/.

[3] James Pinkerton, "20 arrested in immigration raid at Houston Shipley Do-Nuts," Houston Chronicle, April 16, 2008, http://www.chron.com/news/article/20-arrested-in-immigration-raid-at-Houston-1664461.php.

[4] Lofholm, "Fear from Swift plant raid."

[5] Susan Carroll, "ICE delivers hefty fines for paperwork errors," Houston Chronicle, Feb. 20, 2012, http://www.chron.com/default/article/ICE-delivers-hefty-fines-for-paperwork-errors-3344541.php.

[6] Seung Min Kim, "Senate passes immigration bill," Politico, June 28, 2013, http://www.politico.com/story/2013/06/immigration-bill-2013-senate-passes-093530.

[7] PBS Frontline, "Zero Tolerance," Oct. 22, 2019, https://www.pbs.org/wgbh/frontline/film/zero-tolerance/transcript/.

[8] Alec MacGillis, "The Gang That Failed," New York Times Magazine, Sept. 18, 2016, 53-80, https://www.nytimes.com/2016/09/18/magazine/how-republicans-lost-their-best-shot-at-the-hispanic-vote.html.

[9] "Congressman Dan Crenshaw on Border Security, Work Visas and Political Football," Rational Middle podcast, Episode 5, Oct. 23, 2019. http://rationalmiddle.com/podcast-congressman-dan-crenshaw-on-border-security-work-visas-and-political-football/.

Chapter Eight — A Broken System

[1] Tax law: Elizabeth Hull, *Without Justice for All: The Constitutional Rights of Aliens* (Greenwood Publishing, Westport, Connecticut: 1985), 107; Minos's labyrinth: Lok vs. Immigration & Naturalization Service, U.S. Court of Appeals, Second Circuit, 681 F.2d 107 (2d Cir. 1982).

[2] An additional 20,000 visas may be issued for foreign professionals who graduate with a master's degree or doctorate from a U.S. institution of higher learning. "The H-1B Visa Program," Fact Sheet, American Immigration Council, April 2, 2020, https://www.americanimmigrationcouncil.org/research/h1b-visa-program-fact-sheet.

[3] Refugee Processing Center, "Admissions & Arrivals," https://www.wrapsnet.org/admissions-and-arrivals/.

[4] Claire Felter and James McBride, "How Does the U.S. Refugee System Work?" Council on Foreign Relations backgrounder, Oct. 10, 2017, https://www.cfr.org/backgrounder/how-does-us-refugee-system-work.

[5] Maria Sacchetti, "Here's what you need to know about the diversity visa lottery program," The Washington Post, Nov. 1, 2017, https://www.washingtonpost.com/local/immigration/heres-what-you-need-to-know-about-the-diversity-visa-lottery-program/2017/11/01/69f3f422-bf15-11e7-97d9-bdab5a0ab381_story.html?utm_term=.3996cd8e2916.

[6] Robert S. Kaplan, "Where We Stand: Assessment of Economic Conditions and Implications for Monetary Policy," Federal Reserve Bank of Dallas, Aug. 21, 2018, https://www.dallasfed.org/news/speeches/kaplan/2018/rsk180821.

[7] Bob Sechler, "Shortage of Texas construction workers leads to higher costs, delays," Austin American-Statesman, Sept. 7, 2018, https://www.mystatesman.com/business/shortage-texas-construction-workers-leads-higher-costs-delays/U7zN3iaUB6IWb7xUbJgM6O/.

[8] Kim Slowey, "The Dotted Line: The growing perils of using undocumented workers," ConstructionDive, Oct. 29, 2019, https://www.constructiondive.com/news/the-dotted-line-the-growing-perils-of-using-undocumented-workers/565417/.

[9] Mark Erlich, "Construction Workers and the Gig Economy," *Dissent*, University of Pennsylvania Press, Vol. 67, No. 2, Spring 2020, 83-89, doi: https://doi.org/10.1353/dss.2020.0036.

[10] Interviews with Stan Marek, Aug. 11, 2016, and Chuck Gremillion, Jan. 4, 2017.

[11] Joel Rosenblatt and Josh Eidelson, "Uber, Lyft Sued by California in Major Gig-Economy Crackdown," Bloomberg News, May 5, 2020, https://www.bloomberg.com/news/articles/2020-05-05/uber-lyft-sued-by-california-officials-over-driver-benefits?sref=6ouNDd7w.

[12] Ross Ramsey, "Perry: We're not gonna take it," Texas Tribune, March 16, 2009, https://www.texastribune.org/2009/03/16/perry-were-not-gonna-take-it/.

[13] "Unemployment Insurance Weekly Claims," U.S. Department of Labor press release, May 21, 2020, https://www.dol.gov/ui/data.pdf.

[14] "Governor Abbott Requests Release of Federal Unemployment Funds," Texas Governor's Office press release, March 26, 2020, https://gov.texas.gov/news/post/governor-abbott-requests-release-of-federal-unemployment-funds.

[15] This excludes plumbers, electricians and others licensed by the state. Licensing enabled these groups to set standard hourly rates that avoided the wage drain.

[16] "Build a Better Texas," Workers Defense Project and Division of Diversity and Community Engagement at the University of Texas at Austin, January 2013, 46.

[17] Ibid.

[18] "Table 10. Persons Obtaining Lawful Permanent Resident Status by Broad Class of Admission and Region and Country of Birth: Fiscal Year 2018," *2018 Yearbook of Immigration Statistics*, U.S. Department of Homeland Security, Sept. 2019, https://www.dhs.gov/immigration-statistics/yearbook/2018.

Chapter Nine — Beyond Construction

[1] Lena Groeger, "The Immigrant Effect," ProPublica, July 19, 2017, https://projects.propublica.org/graphics/gdp.

[2] Pia Orrenius, "Benefits of Immigration Outweigh the Costs," The Catalyst, (George W. Bush Institute, Spring 2016), http://www.bushcenter.org/catalyst/north-american-century/benefits-of-immigration-outweigh-costs.html.

[3] Alexandre Tanzi, "U.S. 2019 Births Fall for Fifth Consecutive Year to 35-Year Low" Bloomberg News, May 19, 2020, https://www.bloomberg.com/news/articles/2020-05-20/u-s-2019-births-fall-for-fifth-consecutive-year-to-35-year-low?cmpid=BBD052020_OUS&utm_medium=email&utm_source=newsletter&utm_term=200520&utm_campaign=openamericas&sref=b6vN89mJ.

[4] Neel Kashkari, "Immigration is Practically a Free Lunch for America," The Wall Street Journal, Jan. 18, 2018, https://www.wsj.com/articles/immigration-is-practically-a-free-lunch-for-america-1516320376.

[5] Dennis Nixon, "Rhetoric doesn't match border reality," Houston Chronicle, March 12, 2017, A27.

[6] "Protecting American Jobs," Rational Middle Immigration video series, (Episode 5), 0:21, http://rationalmiddle.com/protecting-american-jobs/.

[7] "Tony Payan & Pamela Lizette Cruz on Identifying and Taxing the Undocumented," Rational Middle podcast, Episode 32, June 10, 2020, http://rationalmiddle.com/podcast/episode-32-tony-payan-pamela-lizette-cruz-on-identifying-and-taxing-the-undocumented/.

[8] "Protecting American Jobs," Rational Middle (Episode 5), 2:56.

[9] Simran Walia, "The economic challenge of Japan's aging crisis," *The Japan Times*, Nov. 19, 2019, https://www.japantimes.co.jp/opinion/2019/11/19/commentary/japan-commentary/economic-challenge-japans-aging-crisis/.

[10] Mina Pollmann, "Is Japan Ready to Welcome Immigrants?" *The Diplomat*, Jan. 22, 2020, https://thediplomat.com/2020/01/is-japan-ready-to-welcome-immigrants/.

[11] Antonio Flores, Gustavo López, Jynnah Radford, "2015, Hispanic Population in the United States Statistical Portrait," (Washington, DC: Pew Hispanic Center, Sept. 18, 2017), https://www.pewresearch.org/hispanic/2017/09/18/2015-statistical-information-on-hispanics-in-united-states-trend-data/.

[12] Susan Burhouse et. al, "2015 FDIC National Survey of Unbanked and Underbanked Households," (Washington DC: FDIC, Oct. 20, 2016), 15, https://www.fdic.gov/householdsurvey/2015/2015report.pdf.

[13] Diana Furchtgott-Roth, "The Economic Benefits of Immigration," Manhattan Institute for Policy Research, Feb. 2013, 4-5, https://www.manhattan-institute.org/pdf/ib_18.pdf.

[14] "Illegal Immigration and Education," National Law Review, Nov. 7, 2012, https://www.natlawreview.com/article/illegal-immigration-and-education.

[15] Jeffrey S. Passel and D'Vera Cohn, "Unauthorized Immigrant Totals Rise in 7 States, Fall in 14," Pew Research Center, Nov. 18, 2014, http://www.pewhispanic.org/2014/11/18/unauthorized-immigrant-totals-rise-in-7-states-fall-in-14/.

[16] Susan Edelman and Isabel Vincent, "Flood of illegal immigrants to pour into NYC schools," New York Post, Nov. 12, 2014, http://nypost.com/2014/11/23/city-schools-warned-of-plans-to-enroll-2350-migrant-children/.

[17] "Fast Facts," National Center for Educational Statistics, https://nces.ed.gov/fastfacts/display.asp?id=43.

[18] "Occupational Employment and Wages," U.S. Bureau of Labor Statistics, May 2016, https://www.bls.gov/oes/current/oes472031.htm.

[19] Forest Time, "How Much Money Do You Earn in Construction?" Houston Chronicle, undated, http://work.chron.com/much-money-earn-construction-10719.html.

[20] Phil Galewitz, "Medicaid Helps Hospitals Pay for Illegal Immigrants' Care," Kaiser Health News, Feb. 12, 2013 https://khn.org/news/medicaid-illegal-immigrant-emergency-care/.

[21] Samantha Artiga and Maria Diaz, "Health Coverage and Care of Undocumented Immigrants," Kaiser Family Foundation, July 15, 2019. https://www.kff.org/disparities-policy/issue-brief/health-coverage-and-care-of-undocumented-immigrants/.

[22] Eric Ruark and Jack Martin, "The Sinking Lifeboat," Federation for American Immigration Reform, 2009, http://www.fairus.org/site/DocServer/healthcare_09.pdf?docID=3521.

[23] Lisa Christensen Gee, Matthew Gardner and Meg Wiehe, "Undocumented Immigrants' State & Local Tax Contributions," The Institute on Taxation & Economic Policy, Feb. 2016, https://itep.org/wp-content/uploads/immigration2016.pdf.

[24] Esther Yu Hsi Lee, "No, Undocumented Immigrants Aren't A Burden On The Health Care System," Think Progress, June 24, 2015, https://archive.thinkprogress.org/no-undocumented-immigrants-arent-a-burden-on-the-health-care-system-39560e0bcaf7/.

[25] "Houston Police Chief Art Acevedo on Public Safety and Immigration," Rational Middle podcast, Episode 20, March 4, 2020, https://soundcloud.com/user-706853813/houston-police-chief-art-acevedo-on-public-safety-and-immigration.

[26] Anna Flagg, "The Myth of the Criminal Immigrant," *The New York Times*, March 31, 2018, A10, https://www.nytimes.com/interactive/2018/03/30/upshot/crime-immigration-myth.html.

[27] Jonathan Blitzer, "How the Gang MS-13 Became a Trumpian Campaign Issue in Virginia," The New Yorker, Nov. 6, 2017, https://www.newyorker.com/news/news-desk/how-the-gang-ms-13-became-a-trumpian-campaign-issue-in-virginia.

[28] Jonathan Blitzer, "The Teens Trapped Between a Gang and the Law," The New Yorker, Jan. 1, 2018, https://www.newyorker.com/magazine/2018/01/01/the-teens-trapped-between-a-gang-and-the-law.

[29] "Homeland Security Spending Since 9/11," National Priorities Project, Feb. 28, 2013, https://www.nationalpriorities.org/analysis/2013/homeland-security-spending-since-911/.

[30] "The Burden of a Broken System," Rational Middle of Immigration, Episode 2, Nov 2017, http://rationalmiddle.com/the-burden-of-a-broken-immigration-system/.

[31] "Wage war," The Economist, Aug. 27, 2016, 18, https://www.economist.com/united-states/2016/08/25/wage-war.

[32] Benjy Sarlin, "How America's harshest immigration law failed," MSNBC.com, May 9, 2014, http://www.msnbc.com/msnbc/undocumented-workers-immigration-alabama.

[33] Ed Pilkington, "Alabama immigration: crops rot as workers vanish to avoid crackdown," *The Guardian*, Oct. 14, 2011, https://www.theguardian.com/world/2011/oct/14/alabama-immigration-law-workers.

[34] Sarlin, "How America's harshest immigration law failed."

[35] Flynn Adcock, David Anderson and Parr Rosson, "The Economic Impacts of Immigrant Labor on U.S. Dairy Farms," Center for North American Studies, Texas A&M University, June 2015, http://cnas.tamu.edu/Immigrant%20Labor%20Impacts%20on%20Dairy%20Final.pdf.

Chapter Ten — The Wall

[1] Tal Kopan, "What Donald Trump has said about Mexico and vice versa," CNN, Aug. 31, 2016, http://www.cnn.com/2016/08/31/politics/donald-trump-mexico-statements/index.html.

[2] Jill Campbell, Baker Ripley, speaking at the CHF Forum, July 12, 2017.

[3] United States Border Patrol, "Nationwide Illegal Alien Apprehensions Fiscal Years 1925-2018, https://www.cbp.gov/sites/default/files/assets/documents/2019-Mar/bp-total-apps-fy1925-fy2018.pdf.

[4] "The Wall," Rational Middle Immigration series (Episode 4) 3:45, http://rationalmiddle.com/the-wall/.

[5] "The dragnet and the scissors," The Economist, Feb. 25, 2017, 23-24, https://www.economist.com/united-states/2017/02/23/congress-and-the-courts-will-poke-holes-in-the-presidents-deportation-plans.

[6] Dug Begley, "Local nonprofit's services, model draw national attention," Houston Chronicle, May 13, 2014, http://www.houstonchronicle.com/news/article/Local-nonprofit-s-services-model-draw-national-5475819.php.

[7] Brandi Grissom and Robert T. Garrett, "'I'll put a bullet in your head': Fistfight nearly erupts on final day of contentious legislative session," Dallasnews.com, May 29, 2017, https://www.dallasnews.com/news/texas-legislature/2017/05/29/fistfight-nearly-erupts-final-day-caps-contentious-legislative-session.

[8] Julia Gelatt, "The RAISE Act: Dramatic Change to Family Immigration, Less So for the Employment-Based System," Migration Policy Institute, Aug 2017, http://www.migrationpolicy.org/news/raise-act-dramatic-change-family-immigration-less-so-employment-based-system.

[9] Stuart Anderson, "The Impact of a Point-Based Immigration System on Agriculture and Other Business Sectors," National Foundation for American Policy, Aug 2017, http://immigrationforum.org/wp-content/uploads/2017/08/NFAP-FINAL.pdf.

[10] Ibid.

[11] The Associated Press, "GOP Plan to Slash Legal Immigration Wins Trump's Support," The New York Times, Aug. 3, 2017, https://web.archive.org/web/20170804144655/https://www.nytimes.com/aponline/2017/08/03/us/politics/ap-us-trump-immigration.html.

[12] "A dream deferred," The Economist, Sept. 9, 2017, 25-26, https://www.economist.com/united-states/2017/09/09/donald-trump-ditches-daca.

[13] Josh Dawsey, "Trump derides protections for immigrants from `shithole' countries," The Washington Post, Jan. 12, 2018, https://www.washingtonpost.com/politics/trump-attacks-protections-for-immigrants-from-shithole-countries-in-oval-office-meeting/2018/01/11/bfc0725c-f711-11e7-91af-31ac729add94_story.html?utm_term=.f0f29fa737c9.

[14] Ana Gonzalez-Barrera, "More Mexicans Leaving Than Coming to the U.S.," Pew Research Center, Nov. 19, 2015, http://www.pewhispanic.org/2015/11/19/more-mexicans-leaving-than-coming-to-the-u-s/.

Chapter Eleven — A Better Way

[1] "The Impact of Administration Policies on Immigration Levels and Labor Force Growth," National Foundation for American Policy, February 2020, https://nfap.com/wp-content/uploads/2020/02/Legal-Immigration.NFAP-Policy-Brief.February-2020.pdf.

Chapter Twelve — Stan's Plan

[1] "The Difference Between DACA and the DREAM Act," Immigration Solutions, July 28 2017, https://www.fileright.com/blog/the-difference-between-daca-and-the-dream-act/.

[2] Mark Erlich interview for Rational Middle podcast, unaired, Feb. 12, 2020.

Epilogue

[1] "Immigrant Healthcare Workers on the Front Lines of COVID-19 with Andrew Lim," Rational Middle podcast, Episode 25, April 22, 2020.

[2] Miriam Jordan, "Farmworkers, Mostly Undocumented, Become `Essential' During Pandemic," The New York Times, April 2, 2020, https://www.nytimes.com/2020/04/02/us/coronavirus-undocumented-immigrant-farmworkers-agriculture.html.

[3] Brent Orrell, "Hypocrisy strikes: 'Essential workers' and the meat packing industry," AEIdeas, The American Enterprise Institute, April 29, 2020, https://www.aei.org/poverty-studies/hypocrisy-strikes-essential-workers-and-the-meat-packing-industry/.

[4] William Feuer, "CDC says 3% of workers in surveyed meat processing plants tested positive for coronavirus," CNBC.com, May 1, 2020. https://www.cnbc.com/2020/05/01/coronavirus-cdc-says-3percent-of-workers-in-surveyed-meat-processing-plants-infected.html.

[5] The Associated Press, "Meatpackers Welcome Trump Order; Others Question Virus Risks," The New York Times, April 29, 2020, https://apnews.com/fb38a5a53ac1a92039bc0a4b545b19d7.

[6] Adam Jeffrey, "Wasted milk, euthanized livestock: Photos show how coronavirus has devastated U.S. agriculture," CNBC.com, May 2, 2020, https://www.cnbc.com/2020/05/02/coronavirus-devastates-agriculture-dumped-milk-euthanized-livestock.html.

[7] "Jim Baron on COVID-19's Impact on Restaurants and Immigration," Rational Middle podcast, Episode 23, April 8, 2020.

Selected Bibliography

Bernstein, Patricia. *Ten Dollars to Hate: The Texas Man Who Fought the Klan*, (Texas A&M University Press, College Station, Texas: 2017).

Cantú, Francisco. *The Line Becomes a River: Dispatches from the Border* (Riverhead Books, New York: 2018).

Caplan, Bryan and Zach Weinersmith. *Open Borders: The Science and Ethics of Immigration* (First Second Books, New York: 2019).

Chomsky, Aviva. *"They Take Our Jobs! And 20 Other Myths About Immigration* (Beacon Press, Boston: 2007).

———. *Undocumented: How Immigration Became Illegal* (Beacon Press, Boston: 2014).

Gjelten, Tom. *A Nation of Nations* (Simon & Schuster, New York: 2015).

Golash-Boza, Tanya Maria. Immigrant Nation: *Raids, Detentions, and Deportations in Post-9/11 America* (Paradigm Publishers, Boulder, Colorado: 2012).

Harrigan, Stephen. *Big Wonderful Thing* (The University of Texas Press, Austin, Texas: 2019).

Kleinberg, Stephen. *Prophetic City: Houston on the Cusp of a Changing America* (Simon & Schuster, New York: 2020).

Kolker, Claudia. *The Immigrant Advantage: What We Can Learn from Newcomers to America about Health, Happiness, and Hope* (Free Press, New York: 2011).

Massey, Douglas S., Jorge Durand and Nolan J. Malone. *Beyond Smoke and Mirrors: Mexican Immigration in an Era of Economic Integration*, (Russell Sage Foundation, New York: 2002).

Monty, Jacob. *The Gringo's Guide to Hispanics in the Workplace* (Emporion Press, Miami: 2011).

———. *The Gringo's Guide to Immigration Reform for Employers* (Emporion Press, Miami: 2013).

Okrent, Daniel. *The Guarded Gate: Bigotry, Eugenics, and the Law That Kept Two Generations of Jews, Italians, and Other European Immigrants Out of America*, (Scribner, New York: 2019).

Orner, Peter (ed.). *Underground America: Narratives of Undocumented Lives* (McSweeney's Books, San Francisco: 2008).

Theroux, Paul. *On the Plain of Snakes: A Mexican Journey* (Houghton Mifflin Harcourt, Boston: 2019).

Urrea, Luis Alberto. *The Devil's Highway: A True Story*. (Little, Brown and Co., New York: 2004).

Index

A

B

P

Panama Canal, 39

The Passing of the Great Race, 41, 42

Payan, Tony, 110–11, 129, 130, 143

Pearl Harbor attack, 55

Pelosi, Nancy, 100

Perdue, David, 146

Perry, Rick, 133

Peters, Anna, 37

Peters, Hermina. See Marek, Hermina Peters

Peters, Milady, 38

petrochemical industry, 122

Plyler v. Doe, 132

R

racism, 41, 42, 43–46, 67, 148

RAISE (Reforming American Immigration for Strong Employment) Act, 146, 160

Rational Middle, 21, 178–79

Ray, Alvino, 59

Reagan, Ronald, 80, 81, 103, 142

refugees, 69, 112

Resolution Trust Corporation (RTC), 80

restaurant industry, 175

Rinaldi, Matt, 145–46

Roberts, John, 148

Rodriguez, Jorge, 123

Romero, Ramon, 145

Romney, Mitt, 27, 103

Roosevelt, Theodore, 39

Rubio, Marco, 100

Russian Revolution, 41

S

T

Loren C. Steffy has been a business writer for more than thirty years for publications that include the Houston Chronicle, Bloomberg News, and the Dallas Times Herald. He currently is a writer-at-large for Texas Monthly and a managing director for the communications firm 30 Point Strategies, where he leads the 30 Point Press publishing imprint.

A frequent speaker and commentator on both radio and television, Steffy is the author of *George P. Mitchell: Fracking, Sustainability, and an Unorthodox Quest to Save the Planet; Drowning in Oil: BP and the Reckless Pursuit of Profit; The Man Who Thought Like a Ship;* and, with Chyrsta Castañeda, *The Last Trial of T. Boone Pickens.*

During his journalism career, Steffy was a four-time finalist for the Gerald Loeb Award for Distinguished Business and Financial Journalism, the field's highest honor, and the recipient of numerous state and national awards. His reporting on the collapse of Arthur Andersen was selected for the 2003 edition of the "Best Business Stories of the Year."

Steffy holds a bachelor's degree in journalism from Texas A&M University. He lives in Wimberley, Texas, with his wife, three dogs and an ungrateful cat.

Stan Marek is the president and chief executive officer of the Marek Family of Companies, one of the largest interior contractors in the Southwest. A native Texan, Stan earned a Bachelor of Science degree in finance from Texas A&M University. He began his working career in the drywall industry during summers in high school and continued part-time until completing his tour of active duty with the United States Marine Corps Reserves.

In 1970, Stan worked as a journeyman carpenter and spent the next two years on large commercial projects throughout his hometown of Houston. He then joined Marek Brothers as a project manager, estimator, and sales manager before becoming president in 1982. He was inducted into the Texas A&M's Constructor Hall of Fame in 2015.

Stan is the co-founder of Texans For a Sensible Immigration Policy and the Construction Career Collaborative, which promotes responsible hiring and training practices in the construction industry. He also is a member of the Greater Houston Partnership's task force, Americans For Immigration Reform.

He is a frequent contributor to the Houston Chronicle on immigration reform issues, and he frequently contributes to blogs such as Construction Citizen (*www.constructioncitizen.com*)